Piano Exercises

FOR

DUMMIES®

by David Pearl

WILEY

Wiley Publishing, Inc.

Piano Exercises For Dummies®

Published by
Wiley Publishing, Inc.
111 River St.
Hoboken, NJ 07030-5774
www.wiley.com

Copyright © 2009 by Wiley Publishing, Inc., Indianapolis, Indiana

Published by Wiley Publishing, Inc., Indianapolis, Indiana

Published simultaneously in Canada

For general information on our other products and services, please contact our Customer Care Department within the U.S. at 800-762-2974, outside the U.S. at 317-572-3993, or fax 317-572-4002.

For technical support, please visit www.wiley.com/techsupport.

Wiley also publishes its books in a variety of electronic formats. Some content that appears in print may not be available in electronic books.

Library of Congress Control Number: 2008938380

ISBN: 978-0-470-38765-8

Manufactured in the United States of America

10 9 8 7 6 5 4 3 2 1

About the Author

David Pearl is the author of *The Art of Steely Dan* (Cherry Lane) and *Color Your Chords* (Cherry Lane), a survey of the harmonic styles of 25 top jazz, blues, and rock pianists. He recently completed *The Jazz Piano Collection* (Amsco Publications), twenty-two jazz standards arranged for solo piano, and *The Art of Billy Strayhorn* (Cherry Lane), an in-depth exploration of five songs by one of jazz's greatest composers. His other books include jazz transcriptions of the artists Grover Washington, Jr., Dave Douglas, and Roland Hanna, and arrangements of jazz, classical pieces, and opera arias for piano. A freelance pianist, composer, and arranger, he lives in New York City with his wife and son, and performs and records regularly with singers and other instrumentalists. His new CD, *Scythian Suite*, is a collection of piano four-hands music recorded with his wife, Rubi Miyachi. He developed and recorded a series of piano lessons for the new online music education Web site WorkshopLive. Born in Denver, Colorado, he graduated from the Lamont School of Music at the University of Denver.

Author's Acknowledgments

Thanks to Mark Phillips and Susan Poliniak at Cherry Lane Music for giving me the opportunity to write about, arrange, edit, and engrave music over the years. To Mark, who recommended me to Wiley for this book: More Mondel's chocolate is coming your way.

To Lindsay Lefevere, enthusiastic and supportive acquisitions editor: Thanks for getting me started.

Thanks to Tim Gallan, project editor, for guiding me along this path with his easy-going style.

To Sarah Faulkner, master copy editor, a promise: In the future, my future-tense propensity will be a thing of the past.

Thanks to my son Leon for being my crash-test Dummy, and for making sure my 'Take Me Out to the Ballgame' arrangement passes ballpark muster. (But hold the relish.)

Thanks to my wife, Rubi, the real piano sensei in our family, who agreed to play through every exercise, generously shared her wisdom, gently pointed out problems, and waited for me to complete the five stages of grief before I could see she was, as usual, right.

Thanks to Roxlyn Moret, yogi and hands-on healer, for her careful suggestions for Chapter 1.

Special thanks to David Genova for reviewing this book and making so many important suggestions. You motivated me to tackle the big issues and improve the book all in one move.

Dedication

To my mother, father, and sister, who filled our home with Bach, Brubeck, and The Beatles.

Publisher's Acknowledgments

Weíre proud of this book; please send us your comments through our Dummies online registration form located at `www.dummies.com/register/`.

Some of the people who helped bring this book to market include the following:

Acquisitions, Editorial, and Media Development

Senior Project Editor: Tim Gallan

Acquisitions Editor: Lindsay Lefevere

Senior Copy Editor: Sarah Faulkner

Assistant Editor: Erin Calligan Mooney

Technical Editor: David Genova

Editorial Manager: Michelle Hacker

Editorial Assistants: Joe Niesen, Jennette ElNaggar, David Lutton

Cartoons: Rich Tennant (`www.the5thwave.com`)

Composition Services

Project Coordinator: Erin Smith

Layout and Graphics: Reuben W. Davis, Melissa K. Jester, Christine Williams, Erin Zeltner

Proofreaders: Dwight Ramsey, Shannon Ramsey

Publishing and Editorial for Consumer Dummies

 Diane Graves Steele, Vice President and Publisher, Consumer Dummies

 Joyce Pepple, Acquisitions Director, Consumer Dummies

 Kristin Ferguson-Wagstaffe, Product Development Director, Consumer Dummies

 Ensley Eikenburg, Associate Publisher, Travel

 Kelly Regan, Editorial Director, Travel

Publishing for Technology Dummies

 Andy Cummings, Vice President and Publisher, Dummies Technology/General User

Composition Services

 Gerry Fahey, Vice President of Production Services

 Debbie Stailey, Director of Composition Services

Table of Contents

Introduction

Piano Exercises For Dummies is for people who love playing the piano and want to improve the way they play. I include more than 150 exercises, tips, and explanations to help you gain a greater understanding of your mental and physical approach to the piano. When you combine these exercises with a deeper understanding of how the piano works as an instrument, you can improve the quality of the music you make.

There is a certain paradox in linking exercise with playing the piano: Goals of building muscle strength and developing endurance through repetitive drills, and a "no pain, no gain" mindset don't apply to music making. The awareness that mindless repetition of exercises devoid of musical content and context can be harmful is really the motivating force behind this book. Simply put, you can neither improve nor enjoy playing the piano if you're bored, uncomfortable, or in pain. My goal is to encourage you, the reader, to become more mentally *and* physically engaged as you play. To that end, I include exercises that are fun and have plenty of variation in style, key, and tempo, so that your active participation will lead you to useful discoveries about the way you play the piano.

About This Book

As you glance through the chapter titles either in the table of contents or as you flip through the book, you'll see that you can easily identify the technical skills each chapter addresses. Feel free to go right to a section that attracts your attention. You can pick and choose exercises that address your needs — play some scales, work on your trills, or practice a contrary motion exercise — without playing any of the preceding exercises or reading any of the preceding chapters. As long as you keep in mind the basic approach of feeling comfortable at the piano and keeping mentally engaged while you exercise, you can set this book on your piano at any time and start anywhere you like.

I organize the chapters to follow a typical daily warm-up, starting with individual finger and hand exercises and moving into exercises that involve more of your body and integrate a wide variety of movement at the piano. As an excellent way to use this book, I suggest you pick a few exercises from each chapter as you go through the book, and create an exercise menu that works best for your day.

In most cases, each exercise fits on a single page and directly addresses a specific technical skill; the accompanying text helps explain and explore the technical problem at hand. I composed, arranged, or adapted all the material with the objective of keeping it varied yet consistent, and I engraved all the exercises with the goal of displaying all the notes, fingerings, and articulations as clearly as possible. The exercises avoid mechanical repetition, and I aim to keep things interesting by presenting the material in a variety of melodic, harmonic, and rhythmic settings.

In addition to the techniques most piano exercise books commonly address (finger independence, major and minor scales, chords, octaves, and arpeggios), this book has several special features and additions:

- ✔ Warming up away from the piano, with a section on posture, hand position, and comfortable movement at the keyboard
- ✔ Using the damper pedal
- ✔ Playing ornaments, rolled chords, glissandos, and tremolos

✔ Blues scales, diminished (or octatonic) scales, and chromatic scales

✔ Left-hand accompaniment patterns

✔ Chord progression exercises

✔ Rhythm exercises

✔ Performance pieces at the end of every chapter

✔ Ten extra dance pieces

I encourage you to try different exercises and vary your routine. Use this book to help you stay engaged and involved in your development.

Conventions Used in This Book

These conventions won't seem unfamiliar to you if you're used to reading music:

✔ **Hands-alone and hands-together:** When you see "practice this hands-alone," it means to practice the right- and left-hand parts separately. "Play hands-together" means to play with both hands together.

✔ **Finger numbers:** Finger numbers apply to your fingers in the traditional way — in other words, your thumb is your first (finger one), your index finger is your second (finger two), and so on.

✔ **Fingering:** For the right hand, fingerings are placed above the staff, directly above the notes; for the left hand, fingerings are placed below the staff, directly below the notes.

✔ **Key signatures:** Nearly all the exercises in this book have a simple key signature. Each chapter has a mix of exercises with no flats or sharps and those with one or two sharps or flats.

✔ **Time signatures:** I try to keep a variety of time signatures in rotation throughout the book, but they're all the types you commonly hear and see, including 4/4, 3/4, 2/4, 6/8, and 12/8.

✔ **Performance piece:** Each chapter ends with a performance piece. This is usually a recognizable song or piece adapted from our treasure-filled musical heritage. You can perform these pieces for others or simply enjoy them as your own reward for making it through the chapter.

✔ **Metronome markings:** All performance pieces and some exercises show a metronome marking at the top of the music. These are my *suggested* tempos; always play at a tempo that feels comfortable for you.

What You're Not to Read

If you just want to mine this book for fun and challenging exercises, you're welcome to skip the text and play to your heart's content. The various tips, reminders, and technical advice flagged with a friendly *For Dummies* icon aren't essential to understanding what the exercises are for, so you can skip over them to get to the exercises, but I hope they'll make things even more interesting and fun!

Foolish Assumptions

I made the following assumptions about you when I was writing this book:

- ✔ You picked up this book thinking that you'd sure like to have something new and interesting to play when you warm up.
- ✔ You want to work on your piano skills.
- ✔ You may be feeling that familiar tug on your conscience that says, "I'd really like to improve my piano playing so I could play music I've always wanted to play," or "I sure would love to play the piano more, if I could only find the time."
- ✔ You don't get inspired to do any of the above when you pick up an exercise book and see pages and pages of interminable sixteenth notes.
- ✔ You know how to read notes on the treble and bass staff and count rhythms at a basic level.
- ✔ You may have started taking lessons or have taken some piano lessons in the past.
- ✔ You may have already read *Piano For Dummies* by Blake Neely (Wiley) and are ready for more music.
- ✔ You have access to a piano.

If you're a piano teacher, I assume that you wish you could find something fun and useful for your students to play for warming up and teaching technique. If so, I feel your pain and offer you this book.

If any of my assumptions are true, this book is for you.

How This Book Is Organized

Piano Exercises For Dummies is organized so that you quickly find and play the exercises that fit your needs, desires, or moods. The chapters are grouped into the following five parts, progressing along a typical warm-up sequence.

Part I: Waking Up Your Fingers

This part starts with simple exercises you can do away from the piano to get physically and mentally limber and loose. You review proper posture at the piano to make sure you're as comfortable as possible when you play. In the next two chapters, you exercise the individual fingers of each hand and then work your fingers in different groups and combinations. You focus on finger movement, articulation, and play exercises in a variety of five-finger hand positions.

Part II: Developing a Strong, Supple, and Speedy Hand

In this part you take a look at the different ways you move your hand when you play the piano: Shifting hand positions, using your fingers together as a single unit, and playing chords. You practice finger crossovers and pass-unders, which are essential to shifting hand positions and playing smooth scales and melodic lines, and you learn a comfortable approach to playing chords.

Part III: Including Your Arms and Body

You work on techniques involving a greater range of arm movement in this part. You play a variety of scales up and down a two-octave range, and play exercises with your hands in parallel and contrary motion. A chapter devoted to the use of the damper pedal allows you to examine and improve how you use the pedal while you play. And you work on making jumps across the keyboard, developing a method to make accurate jumps of shorter and longer distances.

Part IV: Integration and Independence

Many of the previous techniques are integrated in more challenging exercises in this part. You get arpeggio exercises combined with hand position changes; finger crossovers combined with arm crossovers; and scales and chords in a variety of rhythmic settings. Rhythm, in fact, is a big feature of this part. You can improve your ability to read and play more difficult rhythms through exercises that challenge you to think ahead, stay engaged with the page, and guide your hands successfully through tricky passages.

You work on chord progressions and cadences, with exercises in a variety of harmonic styles. Ornaments and other fancy techniques are also covered in this part. You play grace notes, trills, and other impressive decorations, and get definitions and explanations to match each ornament.

Part V: The Part of Tens

A favorite feature of any *For Dummies* book, the Part of Tens gives you super-special, no-extra-charge, added bonus information and material. I start off by presenting ten one-page dances to play and satisfy your growing desire to put your newfound abilities to the test. And I give you a list of valuable exercise and étude collections by the greatest composers of piano music so that you can expand your technical horizons.

The CD

All this, and a CD, too?!? You bet. The CD that comes with *Piano Exercises For Dummies* is filled with tracks of me, your humble author, playing many exercises, all performance pieces, and the ten dances (from The Part of Tens). Listen to the CD to hear an example of how the exercises sound, study the way a certain rhythm should be played, enjoy my interpretation of the performance pieces, and inspire you to do your own thing.

Icons Used in This Book

You'll find the following four icons in the left-hand margins throughout this book:

I use this icon to pass along valuable information that may solve a technical problem or simply make playing a certain passage easier.

I use this icon when I want to remind you of the basics: be comfortable, think first, take a break, and so on.

I use this icon to give you technical information and trivia that you may have missed or forgotten while absorbing the hundreds of other details in music lessons when you were a kid.

I use this icon to alert you to a potential problem so that you can avoid injury, pain, or discomfort; stay mentally tuned-in; and watch for an important detail in the music notation.

Where to Go from Here

Not sure where to begin? Chapter 1 is always a good option. Or maybe you want to jump around. Here are a few tips to keep in mind as you start the exercises:

✔ You can custom-make your own daily workout to suit your needs.

✔ The exercises can be effective at a variety of speeds. Adjust the tempo to match your comfort level as well as test your control.

✔ If you find some exercises too difficult, play them hands-alone at first.

✔ For a challenge, transpose an easy exercise up a step, or try to play an exercise written in G in the key of C.

Part I

Waking Up Your Fingers

The 5th Wave

By Rich Tennant

"This exercise is supposed to be played in contrary motion, not irreconcilable motion."

In this part . . .

Before you begin blazing trails over the eighty-eights, make sure your mind and body are simpatico. In this part, you take a little time to warm up your body, monitor any discomfort, release any muscle tension and do a few relaxation and stretching exercises. When you go to the piano, you check out your posture and your body support so you can approach playing the piano in the most comfortable way possible.

As you start in on the exercises, you focus on the movement of each individual finger and how you direct the movement with greater mental participation. As you develop a better awareness of movement at the piano you give yourself the best chance of supporting and controlling your fingers when you play.

Chapter 1

Getting Ready to Practice

- -

In This Chapter

▶ Warming up your body

▶ Relaxing and stretching

▶ Checking your posture at the piano

▶ Moving at the piano

- -

ake a few minutes to warm up and relax your body before you start to practice. Many musicians find that stretches, yoga, the Alexander Technique, and exercise in general help the physical component of playing music by heightening awareness of their bodies and the way they move. After a few stretches and warm-ups, you can bring a relaxed awareness to the piano when you practice.

The warm-ups in this chapter are designed to loosen and relax the areas piano players use the most: the fingers, hands, wrists, arms, shoulders, neck, back, and hips.

Warming Up Away from the Instrument

Why warm up away from the piano? Here are two reasons:

✔ To stretch and release muscles throughout your body from standing positions and floor positions

✔ To develop a routine of feeling loose and comfortable when you go to the piano

Plus, because you can do these warm-ups anywhere and anytime, you can start before you get to your piano.

Releasing tension and releasing your muscles

The basic pattern of tension and release is fundamental to music making, both in the physical process of playing and in the music itself. Playing the piano involves a wide range of movement, from pressing down a key with your fingertip to using your entire upper body in playing scales, arpeggios, and chords. Add in pedaling and you're using your whole body. All this movement requires muscle flexion, extension, and rotation; and movement is enhanced by a fluid, relaxed approach that's unhindered by excess tension in your body. And because piano playing requires so much mental participation along with this physical movement, it's easy to overlook the buildup of tension: gripping in the neck, forearms, and jaw; hunching in the shoulders; and locking the joints in the fingers.

These common manifestations of physical tension can easily become incorporated into your playing through the necessary repetition of practicing. So developing a pattern of releasing your muscles as you play and building this pattern into your playing are very important. Doing this also becomes a way to unify the physical and mental components of music making, because staying comfortable while you play requires constant monitoring for areas of discomfort.

Breathing in an unending circle

Breathing is the model for fluid motion. Think of breathing in an unending circle — the end of an inhalation is the beginning of an exhalation. When you play the piano you want to think of the music, your body, and your mind as part of this constant, fluid motion.

To create the smoothest, most luxurious breathing cycle you can imagine, follow these steps:

1. **Stand with your shoulders and arms relaxed at your side as you develop this slow cycle of inhalation and exhalation.**

2. **Inhale through your nose slowly and evenly, deeply filling your lungs over a smooth arc of time.**

3. **Turn the inhalation into an exhalation without holding your breath, like a swimmer reverses direction in a pool, always in motion.**

4. **Exhale fully, without pushing, and let go of all the air until you're ready to begin another inhalation.**

5. **As you develop this slow cycle, let all your muscles relax and let go in the same rhythm.**

Allow the breath to widen your upper body, back, shoulders, and neck so that you feel as if you're loosening and lengthening throughout your body.

Massaging, stretching, and contracting your hands

Give all your joints, muscles, and bones in one hand a gentle massage with the other hand (see Figure 1-1). Squeeze, rub, stretch — do whatever feels soothing. Start with your wrist bones and work toward the fingertips, thoroughly massaging the top, sides, and bottom of your hand, and then switch to the other hand.

Follow these steps for an effective hand stretch:

1. **Spread your fingers into a comfortably wide span, palms down.**

2. **Contract your hand, bringing your thumb all the way under your pinky so you make an "X" with the thumb and pinky under the other fingers, as shown in Figure 1-2.**

3. **Spread your fingers into a wide span again.**

4. **Contract your hand, making the "X" with your pinky under your thumb, releasing all the way back along the finger joints to the wrist.**

5. **Repeat this exercise a few times, and then try it with your thumb crossing under and then over your fourth, third, and second fingers.**

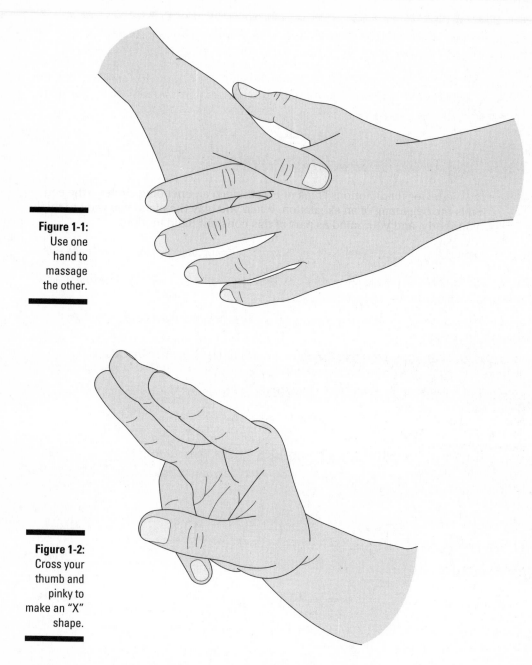

Figure 1-1:
Use one
hand to
massage
the other.

Figure 1-2:
Cross your
thumb and
pinky to
make an "X"
shape.

Continue your warm-up by contracting your hand:

1. **Make a tight fist and wrap your thumb across the outside of fingers two through five (see Figure 1-3).**

2. **Expand all your fingers, with space between each finger in a comfortable stretch.**

3. **Close your fist again, this time with the thumb tucked inside fingers two through five.**

4. **Repeat with both hands, alternating the thumb position.**

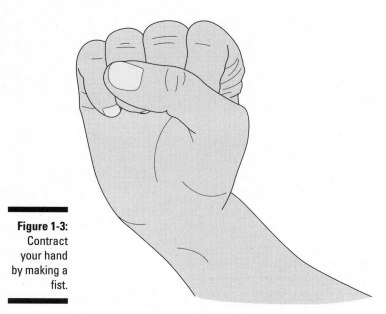

Figure 1-3:
Contract
your hand
by making a
fist.

Warming up your wrists

Give your wrists a warm-up by following these steps:

1. **Hold your hands in front of you, palms facing away, as if to signal "stop" with both hands (see Figure 1-4).**

2. **With a loose wrist, slowly circle your hands both clockwise and counterclockwise.**

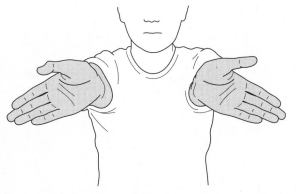

Figure 1-4:
Hold your
hands out
and slowly
move them
in circles.

3. **Bring your hands together in front of you like you're praying, palm-to-palm, finger-to-finger, and extend your elbows out to the side.**

4. **Slowly rotate your wrists so that your fingers point toward you, and then away from you, and finally down to the ground, as shown in Figure 1-5.**

5. **Repeat a few times as you loosen your wrists.**

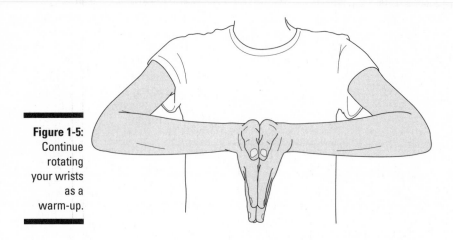

Figure 1-5:
Continue
rotating
your wrists
as a
warm-up.

Swinging and twisting your arms

Try this exercise and then enjoy the looseness you feel throughout your arms:

1. **Swing your forearms up from your elbows to the side to touch your thumb to your shoulder (see Figure 1-6a).**

2. **Let your forearms swing down gently, the momentum extending your arms out behind you but without reaching back (see Figure 1-6b).**

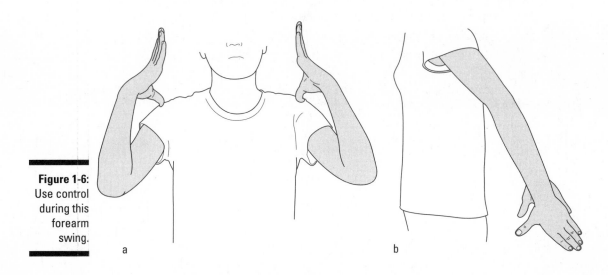

Figure 1-6:
Use control
during this
forearm
swing.

a   b

To continue stretching your arms, follow these steps:

1. **Stand facing a wall, at an arm's length away.**

2. **Reach both arms straight to the wall, at eye level, and put your hands on the wall, fingers pointing up, feeling your entire palm and all fingers firmly against the wall (see Figure 1-7).**

3. **Extend your arms to their fullest extension by taking tiny steps backward.**

4. **Relax and let your arms rest at your side.**

5. **Repeat this stretch, but with the fingers of both hands pointing in toward each other, and then pointing out to the side, and then pointing down to the floor.**

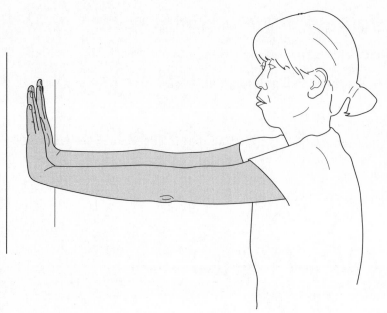

Figure 1-7:
Place your outstretched hands on the wall in front of you.

Finish your arm stretches with this exercise:

1. **Stand perpendicular to a wall with your right side closest to the wall, at arm's length.**

2. **Reach your right arm straight out to the wall and put your hand flat against the wall, fingers pointing up.**

3. **Slowly and gently look left as you extend your right arm into the wall (see Figure 1-8).**

4. **Use your left hand to massage the tight areas around your right shoulder and clavicle.**

5. **Repeat on the other side.**

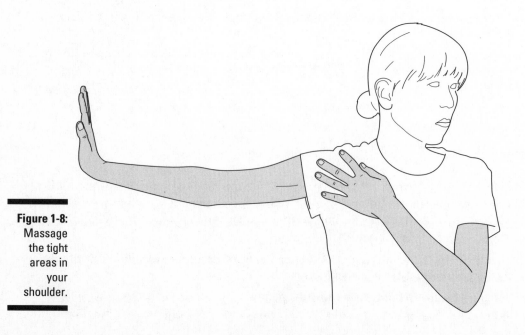

Figure 1-8:
Massage the tight areas in your shoulder.

Stretching your shoulders and neck

To stretch your shoulders and neck, follow these steps:

1. **Stand with your head in a neutral position and your hands at your sides.**

2. **Hunch your shoulders (see Figure 1-9) straight up to chin level, and then release down.**

3. **Circle your shoulders front to back, and back to front as you hunch and release.**

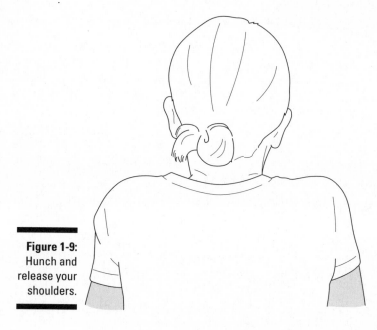

Figure 1-9:
Hunch and
release your
shoulders.

Work on this shoulder and neck warm-up next:

1. **Reach your right hand up and behind your right shoulder to touch the shoulder blade on your right side.**

2. **Bring your left hand behind your back at the waistline, and reach up to touch your right hand.**

   If you can't reach, try dangling a strap, belt, or some other suitable extension so your left hand can grab on (see Figure 1-10).

3. **Repeat these steps with your hands reversed.**

To continue your shoulder and neck stretches, follow these steps:

1. **Grab the top of your head with your right hand and touch the top of your left shoulder with your left hand.**

2. **As shown in Figure 1-11, use your right hand to gently guide your head down to the right, toward your right shoulder.**

3. **At the same time, gently pull down on your left shoulder with your left hand, giving your neck muscles a nice stretch.**

4. **Repeat the stretch on the opposite side.**

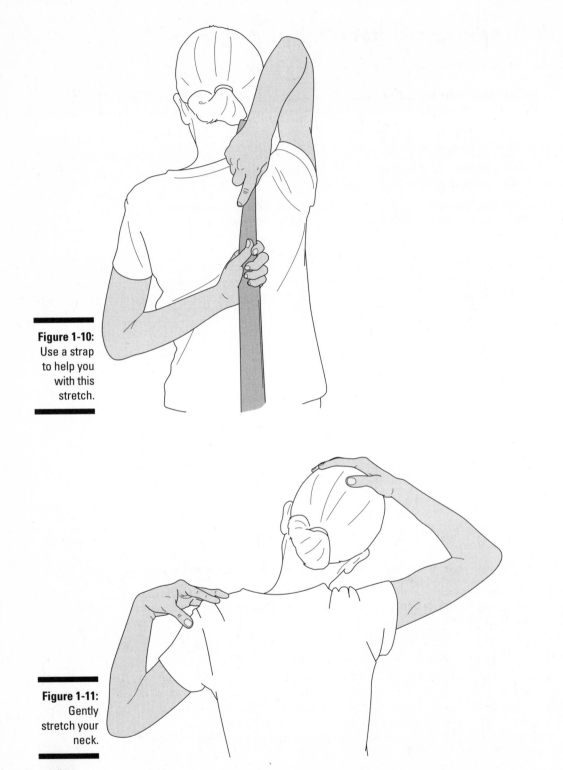

Figure 1-10:
Use a strap
to help you
with this
stretch.

Figure 1-11:
Gently
stretch your
neck.

Keep your stretches in sync with your breathing; your movement should be relaxed and flowing, not stiff and rigid.

Working on your back

The following exercise will stretch your back:

1. **Stand with your feet just a few inches apart, fold your arms in front of you, and cup each elbow with the opposite hand.**

2. **Looking down to the floor, bend your knees and squat down, and let your elbows reach toward the floor in front of your feet.**

3. **Lower your head forward so you're looking at your knees and your back is nicely rounded (see Figure 1-12).**

4. **Slowly rise up, still holding your elbows and bringing your arms up above your head to reach, lengthen, stretch, and widen your back.**

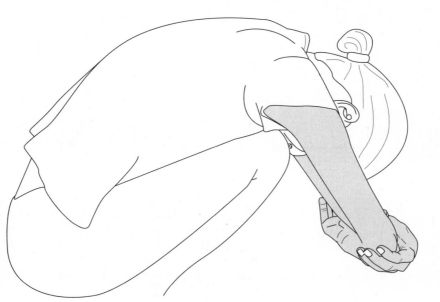

Figure 1-12:
Round your
back before
reaching up
to stretch.

If you want to do more back stretches, I recommend two yoga poses that are excellent for your back: Cat Pose and Child's Pose. For more on these and other poses, check out _Yoga For Dummies,_ by Georg Feuerstein, Larry Payne, and Lilias Folan (Wiley).

Stretching your hamstrings

Sitting can be a lot of work! Tight hamstrings can make it difficult for you to sit at the piano because the tight muscles pull down on the back of the pelvis, which means you have to do a lot of work to get your upper body balanced on your sitting bones. (You'll read more about this in the next section.) So stretch those hamstrings, too, by following these steps:

1. **Keep your legs and back straight as you stand and bend at the waist.**

2. **Reach with your arms to the floor to stretch your hamstrings.**

   If you can't reach the floor, reach down to a piano bench or low table placed in front of you (see Figure 1-13).

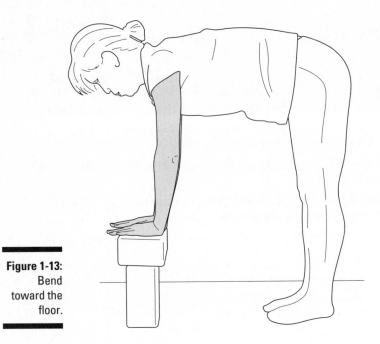

Figure 1-13:
Bend
toward the
floor.

Perfecting Practice with Proper Posture

Start with a common-sense approach to your posture: Aim to situate yourself comfortably in a stable, balanced position so you can play and read music, with room to move freely. The trouble is, piano players can get so caught up in the complication of notes, clefs, fingering, rhythms, and dynamics that they often forget about their bodies. So a reminder to monitor your comfort level and make appropriate adjustments is always a good thing.

Sitting at the piano: Height and angle

If you're too close to the piano, you cramp up your arms and scrunch your shoulders. If you're too far away, you overreach, putting stress on those parts (the neck, upper arm, and pelvic support) that have to work to support your overextended parts. You want to feel comfortably loose, with enough room to move freely and enough support to feel light and long in the upper body and head. You should be able to move easily in either direction of the keyboard, just enough to follow and support your arms when they venture away from the middle to the high or low registers.

Check that your bench or chair is the right height. A common way to measure this is by seeing that your elbows are even with the height of the keyboard when you're sitting at the piano with your hands in playing position. You should see a slight arc from the elbow to the top of your wrist and back down your hand to the keyboard. You have a big advantage if you use an adjustable bench or chair (available on the Web at places like www.cpsimports.com and www.pianobench.com). The benches that come with most pianos aren't a comfortable height for many people. If you don't want to buy an adjustable chair or bench, a typical kitchen chair is a good alternative.

Good posture is all about support. Think about building support from the ground up:

1. **With the floor and the bench or chair providing your support base, align your body so your torso, shoulders, neck, and head are fully supported from underneath.**

2. **With both feet on the floor, and with your knees directly above your feet, sit evenly on your sitting bones so you feel a strong, stable support for your upper body.**

3. **Don't let your weight fall back; bring the back of your pelvis (your hip bones on the sides and sacrum in the back) up above the sitting bones, and continue this line of support up through your spine to the top of your head.**

   Your spine has four curves; it takes careful awareness and support in both the front and back to balance and feel centered throughout your upper body.

4. **Keep your head supported above your spine; don't let it drop or lean in any direction.**

   If you're hunching, slouching, or leaning, you're going to have to use your muscles and energy to compensate for the imbalance.

5. **Release your shoulders if they're holding any tension, and let your arms hang to the side.**

6. **As you breathe in, feel the full length of your upper body from the sitting bones to the top of your head.**

7. **Breathe out and feel a relaxed, stable balance throughout your body.**

Getting a handle on proper hand position

Your hands should feel supported by your shoulders and arms, balanced and relaxed so they can move as easily as possible. Your wrist should be high enough that your fingers make a slightly curved shape with the fingertips on the keys, but not so high that you restrict movement. You should see a rounded shape created by the soft, relaxed undersides of your fingers and palm, similar to the shape of your hand draped around the fist of the other hand, as shown in Figure 1-14.

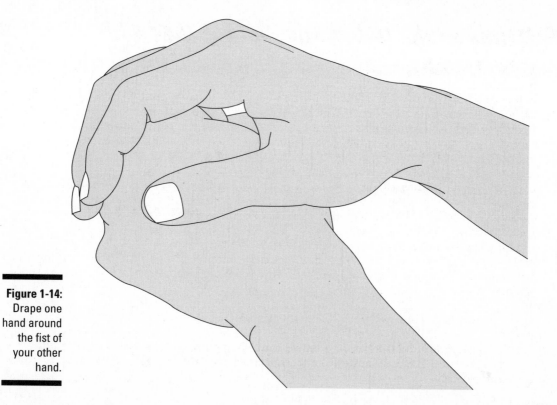

Figure 1-14:
Drape one hand around the fist of your other hand.

As you move up and down the keyboard, try to keep this shape and feeling, with a minimum of twisting at the wrist.

Hands on the fallboard: Counting out loud and bouncing

Close the fallboard over the piano keys, and place your hands in playing position, as I describe in the previous section. With your fingertips touching the top of the fallboard, count out a steady, moderate, four-beat pattern of eighth notes, "one, and, two, and, three, and, four, and . . ." (see Figure 1-15). With a smooth motion, lightly bounce your wrists down on the beats and back up on the "ands" between the beats.

Figure 1-15: Count these eighth-notes.

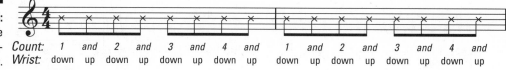

You're creating a model for playing the piano in tempo; remember this model when you play the exercises in this book and any other music. You're counting and moving with the beat, your wrists are free and loose, and your fingers are in a nice, rounded shape. Incorporate this model into your fluid motion cycle, reading music and playing the piano in the motion of tempo and the musical phrase. The combination of reading music, counting, and playing on the keyboard in a steady, continuous tempo may sound complex, but it's easier and more musical when you incorporate all the elements into one activity.

Hands on the fallboard: Hand arches and finger drops

The next exercise gives you practice switching comfortably from a contracted, arched hand position to an open hand position with your fingers loosely extended. To do the exercise, follow these steps:

1. **Let your hands rest, palms down, on top of the fallboard.**

2. **Raise your wrists as you touch your fingertips together in a point, fingers extended and still touching the wood (see Figure 1-16).**

3. **Spread your fingers and let your wrists drop easily until your palms are on the fallboard again.**

4. **Repeat several times.**

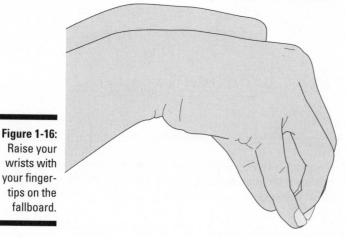

Figure 1-16:
Raise your
wrists with
your finger-
tips on the
fallboard.

Hands on the fallboard: Rotation in and out, movement up and down the keyboard

The next exercise gives you an example of how small forearm rotation should feel. You use this motion when playing broken-chord figures like the Alberti bass pattern in Chapter 11. To do a rotation exercise, follow these steps:

1. **Start with your hands in playing position, fingertips on the wood, wrists fairly high (see Figure 1-17).**

2. **Rotate your wrist slowly to the left, and then to the right, feeling the weight transfer across your entire hand, through your wrist, knuckles, and fingertips.**

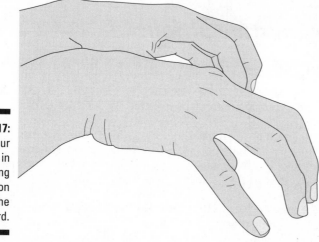

Figure 1-17:
Put your
hands in
playing
position on
top of the
fallboard.

To get a feel for the motion up and down the keyboard — which is what you want when you play the scales in Chapter 7 — try this exercise:

1. **Start with your hands in playing position, fingertips on the wood.**

2. **Move your hands, forearms, and elbows evenly out to the sides and back in, keeping them all on the same plane, as if they were riding on a lateral-moving elevator (see Figure 1-18).**

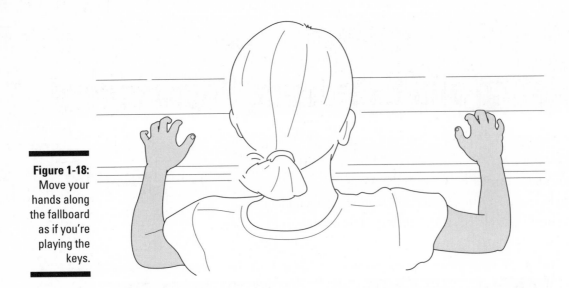

Figure 1-18:
Move your hands along the fallboard as if you're playing the keys.

Hands on the keyboard: Sound and movement on the keys

After completing the exercises in the previous sections, lift the fallboard to see those 88 keys eagerly awaiting your tingling fingers. You have to be willing to make some unusual music for this exercise, but give it a try: Playing and missing any notes that happen along the way, do the wrist bounces, hand arches and finger drops, wrist rotations, and lateral-movement exercises on the keys. Just try to maintain the position, support, ease of movement, and relaxed feeling you develop throughout this chapter.

Overcoming other posture pitfalls

Be on the lookout for signs of tension: Hunching or muscle grabbing in the shoulders and arms; facial tics (biting or grimacing, clenching in the jaw); and stiffness in the neck or fingers. These points of tension may be indirectly caused by inadequate support, but you can ease them by including them in the larger cycle of tension and release — your fluid motion cycle.

When you release tension, you clear a path for your mind to guide the search for solutions to your technical problems. Technical problems don't get solved by playing a passage over and over, hoping to get it right one time, but by engaging your mind to consider changes and adjustments, examine the results, and lead your body toward new solutions.

Be careful when the instrument may be part of the problem. For example, you may be sitting too low or high on a bench or chair that you can't adjust; a piano action may require extra work; a piano may produce inadequate tone; or you may have an electronic piano without weighted action. You may want to limit practice time and take more frequent breaks if you find yourself in an uncomfortable situation!

If you use an electronic keyboard and/or a digital piano, be especially careful not to injure yourself while playing. Turning down the volume to a very low level to avoid disturbing family, friends, and neighbors can lead you to compensate by over-pounding so you can hear yourself play. Instead, use headphones or earbuds with the volume adjusted to a level similar to what you experience in normal piano playing.

Chapter 2

Isolating and Exercising Your Fingers

In This Chapter

▶ Supporting and controlling each individual finger

▶ Exercising in groups of two-, three-, and four-finger combinations

▶ Playing a performance piece with a melodic line in each hand

Have you ever wished you had complete control of all your fingers when you play the piano, and complete control over dynamics and speed? If you have, join the club. But take a look at your hand, and then at the keyboard. It's not a natural fit, to say the least. All your fingers are a different length, and each finger has a different set of muscles and a different way to make the keys on the piano go down. Your fingers get exercise every day when you write, beckon, grasp, shake, wave, twiddle, and point. (Not to mention your repeat renditions of "Itsy-Bitsy Spider" for the kids.) But when you put your hands on the keyboard, your fingers need some extra help to make the music you want to make.

Developing control and agility starts with isolating each finger so you can learn how each one moves as you strike a key. And if you're a little wary, not to worry: By giving your brain information on each finger, you allow it to figure out how to move the fingers the way you want them to move. The secret is that you can get around your limitations with a little brainpower.

Finger strength comes with freedom of movement. When you tense, or hold, your muscles, you restrict your movement. So you want your fingers to feel comfortable. But they also need support. After you develop firm joints in the fingers and give each finger the support of your hand, wrist, arm, and on through the body, the strength will come from the movement itself. (You can read more about hand position in Chapter 1.)

The exercises in this chapter are combined so you can exercise your fingers in groups of twos, threes, and fours. Exercises for the left hand come first so you don't neglect it. Each exercise challenges your control by starting with eighth-note patterns and changing to triplet and then sixteenth-note patterns.

By the end of the chapter you'll be warmed-up for the performance piece, "Come Back to Sorrento," arranged in the style of a two-part invention.

Two-Finger Exercises for the Left Hand

When doing these exercises, don't start out too fast. Even though you begin with eighth-notes, you have to stay in the same tempo when you get to the triplets and sixteenth notes. Adjust the tempo until you're comfortable playing the sixteenths and start from there.

Exaggerate the articulations and dynamics as you practice and improve. The more you can emphasize the difference in note length and volume, the more you're in control.

Play the two-note slurs in the last two measures with an easy, down-up motion starting in the wrist. Keep your hand shape nice and round throughout, especially for the outside fingers, four and five.

Don't cheat the beat! Make sure you give quarter notes their full value. It's tempting to cut the beat short so you can get on to playing more notes. Better to count the full beat while feeling a relaxed and fluid motion in your hand.

Fingers one and two (left hand)

Fingers two and three (left hand)

Fingers three and four (left hand)

Fingers four and five (left hand)

Two-Finger Exercises for the Right Hand

These exercises are similar to the previous exercises for the left hand, but with a bit more movement in the fingers to increase your flexibility where you'll need it.

Fingers one and two (right hand)

Fingers two and three (right hand)

Fingers three and four (right hand)

Fingers four and five (right hand)

Three-Finger Exercises for the Left Hand

Add a finger, get more melody. You can also add a bit of your own shading to the phrases by trying legato and staccato articulation. Shape each phrase with dynamics you choose to make the most music.

Fingers one, two, and three (left hand)

Fingers two, three, and four (left hand)

Fingers three, four, and five (left hand)

Three-Finger Exercises for the Right Hand

Because you use your right hand to play melodies most of the time, it's important to practice playing melodically. These exercises give you a chance to work on *singing* with your fingers. Shape the melodic phrases as if you were singing them by adding some of your own fine-tuned dynamics. For example, increase the volume on a steadily rising phrase and decrease the volume on a descending phrase.

Fingers one, two, and three (right hand)

When you find your thumb on a black key, look to see that you're touching the edge of the key and aren't sliding in more than you need to. Angle your thumb down from your nicely arched hand.

Fingers two, three, and four (right hand)

Fingers three, four, and five (right hand)

Four-Finger Exercises for the Left Hand

As you try these exercise patterns across your hand, you may hear that the notes played with fingers four and five sound softer than those played with fingers two and three. Keep your hand shape nice and round throughout these exercises, especially for the outside fingers, four and five. Make sure you don't collapse in the finger joints closest to your fingertips or the wrists when you play notes with these fingers.

You can increase the loudness of each note by increasing your attack speed — a faster speed of attack will get a louder sound. By making sure fingers four and five have good shape and support, you make it easier to match attack speeds in all your fingers.

Fingers one, two, three, and four (left hand)

Fingers two, three, four, and five (left hand)

Four-Finger Exercises for the Right Hand

Be sure to give plenty of expression with your right hand — exercises don't have to sound monotonous! For practice, play one phrase soft, the next one louder, and see whether you can control the dynamics at your liberty.

Fingers one, two, three, and four (right hand)

Fingers two, three, four, and five (right hand)

Performance Piece: "Come Back to Sorrento"

In this arrangement, the melody of the song starts in the left hand and moves to the right hand when the key changes from A minor to A major. This gives you an opportunity to make dynamic contrasts between the melody in one hand and the countermelody in the other, as well as gradations within each part. Try bringing the melody out front by playing it a little louder, or by playing the countermelody a little softer.

Ernesto De Curtis

Chapter 3

Music for Five Fingers

. . . .

In This Chapter

▶ Developing stronger articulation skills

▶ Exercising with five-finger scales

▶ Exercising hands-together

▶ Playing your own Paganini variation

. . . .

In this chapter you exercise all the fingers together on each hand, first separately and then together. The exercises will help you develop the control you need to balance and shape melodic lines in each hand.

In the first two sections, you work on developing a greater command of articulation — playing legato lines more smoothly and playing staccato phrases with clean, crisp precision. You focus on exactly how to move to get the most expression with the least amount of work. Then you start to exercise in a variety of five-finger hand positions: major scale, minor scale, extended whole-tone scale, and contracted chromatic scale positions. After you work both hands separately, you play exercises with your hands together.

Have you heard of the Italian violinist Niccolo Paganini, who blazed a path to stardom with his speed and dexterity? He wrote a violin piece that other composers have used as a theme for their own virtuosic flights. At the end of this chapter, it's your turn to burn up the keys with a variation all your own. The performance piece combines the articulations and five-finger-position scale runs from the exercises in an arrangement of Paganini's famous theme.

Niccolo Paganini (1782–1840), violin virtuoso, was known for a level of technical skill not seen on the concert stage at the time. He wrote music to feature his wizardry, including his Caprice No. 24, which has a theme that many other composers have used as a take-off point for their own variations. The best known of these are Brahms, Rachmaninoff, and Liszt. Composer Witold Lutoslawski (1913–1994) also wrote variations on this theme, to be played by two pianists on two pianos!

Smooth Articulation: Playing Legato

The goal of playing legato is to play all the notes inside a legato slur smoothly and evenly, without any break in the melodic line as you play note to note. To practice this, go for an overlap from one note to the next, finger-to-finger. Play the first note, and then overlap by releasing the key just after the next note sounds. You can exaggerate this at first, so you can hear both notes sounding at the same time; then minimize the overlap to the point where you're satisfied with a smooth legato transition from one note to the next. Listen to the overall phrase, and make slight changes in loudness within the phrase to give it a nice shape.

Legato exercise for the right hand

Legato exercise for the left hand

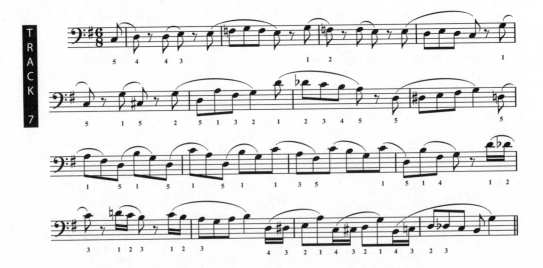

Short Articulation: Playing Staccato

Your goal here is to make every staccato eighth note the same length, and that length should be short! One way to do this is to create the same amount of "space" between each staccato note. Listen for the space between the notes as much as you listen to the notes themselves. You'll find that by keeping a firm joint on each finger, you can quickly lift your hand straight up off the keyboard as you release each note. As you play faster passages and faster tempos, you can minimize this move until the key release is only at the fingertip.

Staccato exercise for the right hand

Staccato exercise for the left hand

Developing Right-Hand Finger Independence with Five-Finger Position Scales

Time to work by playing notes within a five-note hand position, changing positions as you change phrases. These exercises are good for testing your speed and control. Try playing these faster and slower to find out where you lose control. Is it one finger in particular? At a certain tempo? After you find your limits, practice within them and expand them step-by-step.

These exercises begin with two eighth-note pickups. When you start a phrase with a pickup, think of the pickup notes as moving toward the downbeat, with a bit of emphasis on the downbeat itself.

Major: In sequence, out of sequence

Minor: In sequence, out of sequence

Whole tone: In sequence, out of sequence

Chromatic: In sequence, out of sequence

Developing Left-Hand Finger Independence with Five-Finger Position Scales

Left-hand scales can be more challenging because you get more practice time playing melodic phrases with the right hand. Stay within a tempo that you feel you can comfortably control.

Major: In sequence, out of sequence

Minor: In sequence, out of sequence

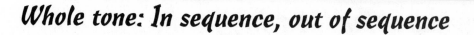

Whole tone: In sequence, out of sequence

Chromatic: In sequence, out of sequence

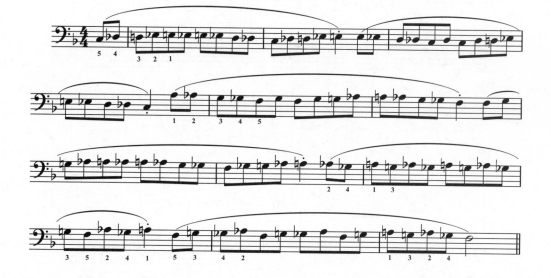

Doubling the Fun: Putting the Hands Together

Right-hand and left-hand parts share the same rhythm in these exercises so you can match the articulation and dynamics as closely as possible. If you notice that one hand sounds weaker than the other, practice hands separately with the stronger hand first, and follow right after with the weaker hand so it can "copy" the stronger one.

Legato articulation, five-finger positions

Staccato articulation, five-finger positions

Performance Piece: Paganini Variation for Ten Fingers

In this piece, your hands move from one five-finger position to another. Spend some time plotting out when the positions change and how far the moves will be. This way, your mind is engaged and in control, directing your hands from position to position. As you become more familiar with the moves, you can increase your speed.

TRACK 9

Moderately fast ♩ = 108

Part II
Developing a Strong, Supple, and Speedy Hand

The 5th Wave   By Rich Tennant

"Okay – I'll front the band. But I want someone other than Dopey on piano."

In this part . . .

You start to move your hand over more and more keyboard territory and build your chord playing skills. Traversing the keyboard means working on fundamental finger moves: crossing a finger over and passing a finger under another finger to shift hand positions. The chord work in this part starts with practice moving two fingers together as a single unit, playing two notes at the same time. Then you move on to three-note chord exercises that take you through a series of steps to ensure comfortable, solid chord playing while releasing any muscle tension.

Chapter 4

Passing Under and Crossing Over

. . . .

In This Chapter

▶ Working on the mechanics of getting around the keyboard

▶ Smoothing your traversing technique

▶ Extending the scale beyond five-finger position

▶ Playing a performance piece with scale runs

. . . .

*O*ne of the biggest challenges in developing a good technique is smoothing out the transitions as you move your hands up and down the keyboard. Imagine playing fluid lines, shifting hand positions seamlessly, and covering the keyboard territory with flexible fingering. You often hear people say, "They make it look easy," when they watch great piano players. That's because great piano players have figured out how to make it easy for themselves.

Before Bach's time, keyboard players avoided using their thumbs, which must have resulted in some really awkward fingerwork, I'd say. Adding the thumb means you can play more notes within one hand position, but the problem remains that the thumb has a very different size, shape, and angle when compared with the other fingers. If you run out of fingers when the melodic line continues up or down, you have to move your hand position, and do it without breaking the musical line. The two best options are to pass the thumb under or cross the other fingers over.

The keyboard terrain sets up different scenarios for these transitions, with possibilities available in the various white and black key combinations. Because the thumb is shorter, the easiest way to cross over it or pass it under is with a black-white combination, because you can use the key height and location to your advantage. With one of your long fingers on a black key you naturally elevate your hand, like a bridge, for your thumb to pass under. With your thumb on a white key, it's easier to cross a long finger over if it's reaching for a black key. It's more difficult to pass or cross from white key to white key because you have less room to pass under and farther to cross over. These more difficult transitions can cause you to twist your hand position, flare out your elbow, tuck in your elbow, or otherwise contort yourself as you move up or down the keyboard, and the extra movement can get in the way of playing smoothly and comfortably.

The answer is to keep your hand quiet, and keep your arm perpendicular to the keyboard as you move out to the extremes or into the middle. This will make your scale runs sound smooth and feel more comfortable. But making these traverses seamless does take practice. The exercises in this chapter give you practice crossing over and passing under with different finger combinations, using a variety of scales. You also discover how to make these transitions more comfortable.

The performance piece at the end of the chapter showcases your smooth scale runs. It's an arrangement of an aria from the opera *La Cenerentola* (Cinderella) by Rossini.

One Under Two, Two Over One

You first want to find a hand shape that eases the transition from one hand position to the next. Start by making a rounded "O" shape with fingers one and two. It helps to keep the two fingertips relatively close together and the top of your hand raised high but still flat. Now feel your fingertips on each key as you play the exercise. Make sure you're not flattening your thumb or hitting the key with the side of your thumb. Similarly, watch that you're not overextending your second finger; you want to come down on the key with the center of your fingertip. You may find it easier to straighten your second finger a bit as it crosses over your thumb to play a black key and curve it a bit when it plays a white key. You can apply this to your third and fourth finger in the following exercises.

One Under Three, Three Over One

Work on smoothing out your hand movements with this exercise. Keep your hand position quiet, and watch for any unnecessary twisting. Moving sideways smoothly, make sure you don't collapse your wrist when you pass your thumb under. You can hear when this happens, because the notes you play with the thumb stand out with a "thunk."

If you play a note unintentionally louder or softer than others, or too early or late, you may have lost control of the attack speed and timing. You can control the volume of a note if you think ahead to plan a hand shape that allows control of the attack speed. You can control your timing by guiding your fingers to perform a smooth movement.

One Under Four, Four Over One

This finger combination is more challenging because you need to contract your hand fully for the position shift and still make it sound smooth and effortless. Watch your fingers once as they make the shift: Is your thumb or fourth finger aiming too far? Often you can cut down on the movement by making sure the crossing/passing finger hits the nearest spot on the key to strike it comfortably. Try watching your fingers carefully to see whether you're overreaching.

Remember to relax! When you're contracting your hand or reaching over and under, make sure you're not locking up, or holding, in any of your joints — especially the thumb. Feel an easy, fluid motion as you move.

Extending Scales with Crossovers and Pass-Unders

Now you can combine the crossing and passing practice you've done in the following two exercises with extended scale runs. Exercise slower to focus on smooth transitions, and faster to focus on lightness and agility.

C- and G-major scale passages

B-flat and F-major scale passages

Performance Piece: Aria from La Cenerentola

The charming character of this aria is well suited to polishing your graceful scale runs and light, staccato touch. Try singling out the sixteenth-note scale runs to practice the cross-overs and pass-unders before you play the piece. Make as much contrast as you can between the staccato and legato, and remember that the rests can be as important as the notes.

Chapter 5

Playing Intervals

In This Chapter

▶ Playing two notes at the same time

▶ Focusing on finger placement and timing

▶ Exercising finger combinations with greater control

▶ Playing a piece with intervals in both hands

playing piano can be like having a choir at your fingertips. You have a ten-member group, some are shorter and some are taller, some like to show off and some prefer to blend in, and one or two really don't take well to being singled out. As the conductor of the fingertip chorale, you have control over how each "voice" in your choir responds to your direction. You can bring up the bass, hush the choir while the soprano has a solo, or lift up every voice for the full-out finale.

This chapter gives you some exercises to gain command over each finger combination so that when you're playing two notes together you have the strength and control to balance and blend. These interval exercises also let you scrutinize the many combinations of fingers, intervals, and positions on the keyboard to get to know how each finger responds. Special attention is given to strengthening those fingers that need it the most, but we try not to embarrass those fingers in front of the others!

When you're done with these exercises you can bring the same approach to playing chords in the next chapter. You'll be adjusting the balance of things, fine-tuning your touch as you play.

Playing Seconds with Different Finger Combinations

Seconds are any interval combination on adjacent keys, white or black. Because of the keyboard layout, that means a variety of hand and finger positions to work on.

Each of the finger combination exercises in this section includes a study for the right hand and the left hand separately. Play through these exercises a few times slowly at first — concentrating on each hand — listening carefully to adjust the balance and timing of each finger combination. Curve your fingers and keep the finger joints firm to play the seconds evenly. Then gradually increase your speed each time you play the exercise. As you increase your speed and accuracy, play this section as a series, starting with the right and left hand in the first finger combination, moving on to the right and left hand in the next finger combination, and so on.

As you play the seconds with each finger combination, imagine the two fingers moving together as one unit. In the first combination, for example, finger two and finger three move together to strike each interval in a synchronized motion.

Finger combination: Two and three

Start with two of your most agile fingers, your second and third fingers. Adjust your attack and your timing to play the seconds evenly while changing hand positions.

Finger combination: Three and four

Try to eliminate excess movement by keeping your hand close to the keyboard.

Finger combination: One and two

You may find playing the seconds evenly difficult to do with this finger combination. Your first two fingers are such different lengths! Bring your fingertips close together, like you're forming an "O," before striking the keys.

Finger combination: Four and five

Work on building strength in your fourth and fifth fingers by keeping the joints firm to make the accents strong.

Playing Thirds with Different Finger Combinations

These exercises improve your agility as you maneuver both major and minor thirds. The different finger combinations keep all your fingers nimble so you can use all five fingers more confidently.

Finger combination: One and three

Take a look at your hand position as you get ready to play. Make sure you have a nice, high arch to your hand, and let your fingers hang down and your fingertips lightly touch the keys.

Finger combination: Two and four

This next exercise is a good one to play with both staccato and legato articulation.

Finger combination: Three and five

Work for an even sound; balance the thirds so the two notes are the same volume. And make sure your thumb stays relaxed and isn't playing louder than the other fingers.

Finger combinations: One and four, two and five, one and five

Here's your "Mt. Everest" exercise for the thirds. Keep your wrists up high, and lift your fingers up like spider legs, bringing them down evenly in twos. And not too fast on this one — taking it slow and developing control are fine; stay relaxed and melt into the keys.

Playing Fourths with Different Finger Combinations

Practicing fourths is really good for finger independence. The different finger combinations keep your muscle coordination sharp.

Finger combinations: One and four, two and five

This one is especially good for the fourth finger. Work on keeping it curved, and prepare it directly above the key that it's going to strike. If you feel like giving yourself a challenge, try to play both hands at the same time!

Finger combinations: One and three, one and two

You're stretching out into a wider hand position here. Check that you're maintaining a good shape in your fifth finger, that it's not flat as it reaches to play its note. You can give your pinky some help by letting go of the fourth interval and moving your hand out, keeping the arched shape, toward the pinky.

Playing Fifths, Sixths, and Sevenths

As you exercise these larger intervals, you also get good preparation for chord playing, which is covered in Chapter 6. Your hand is open wider and you're moving your hand across the keyboard while maintaining a nice, rounded hand shape. The overall goal here is to watch for unnecessary twisting from side to side.

Exercise in fifths

12/8 time is counted as 12 eighth notes to a measure, with each eighth note getting one count. Each measure can have a rhythmic pattern of four strong beats, on one, four, seven, and ten, with three eighth notes inside each strong beat.

You may not think about it so much, but your shortest fingers are the pinky and the thumb, and they're so important in piano playing. Keep both five and one pointing down into the keys — don't collapse the high-arch shape you've been working on! And keep your wrist loose and supple so you're not holding any tension there.

Exercise in fifths and sixths

As you play this exercise, four and five are round, but not stiff. Give these fingers some power and flexibility by bouncing your wrist lightly: "down-up, down-up" as you count "one-and, two-and . . ."

Are you rushin'? Make sure you're not getting faster and faster as you play the exercises. Try turning on the metronome to check your steady speed.

Exercise in fifths, sixths, and sevenths

Give this exercise a bluesy rhythmic feel with a fairly deep wrist bounce on the strong beats in 12/8 time. (That's one, four, seven, and ten.)

Performance Piece: "Take Me Out to the Ballgame"

This familiar old ballpark favorite is arranged with — you guessed it — different interval combinations in each hand. Play each interval pair by using a single, confident hand move, with the same gusto you have when you sing out the tune from the bleachers.

Waltz ♩ = 126

Jack Norworth and Albert Von Tilzer

TRACK 17

Chapter 6

Playing Chords Without Tension

Chord playing is one of the greatest pleasures — and biggest advantages — of playing the piano. The piano sounds best when you make the most of its full harmonic potential.

To get your piano to really sing out, you need flexibility in the wrist to increase your attack speed when you play chords. To balance, or voice, the chord notes, you need control in your fingers to vary the quality of your touch. Naturally, you want to dig into the big chords and get your hands around the really fat harmonies, but keeping stiff fingers and awkward hand positions is tiring and can potentially cause some physical problems. Avoiding these problems and improving your chord voicing are the benefits of learning how to relieve the tension in your fingers, hands, and arms.

This chapter helps you learn to play chords with a relaxed approach, gain a better chord technique, and improve your sound. You can use the exercises to develop fluid motion and release muscle tension as part of a cycle to practice with each chord. The exercises start with single chords, move into a variety of chord progressions, and then combine melody with chords. You finish up with a performance piece that lets you set the room resonating with vibrant chords.

Chord Relaxation

The most important thing to do is make sure you don't hold tension in your hands, arms, and body when you play chords. You do need a certain amount of muscle tone and firmness in the finger joints to play nice, solid chords, but you also want to build in the habit of releasing tension while you play. As you exercise, monitor your body for any area in which you may be holding tension — your arms, shoulders, neck, or even your face (in the form of a grimace or facial tic). Your aim is to breathe through your body as you play and to establish a cyclical pattern of tension and release.

A simple two-chord progression

Start with this simple two-chord progression, and put the following steps into a cycle for each chord:

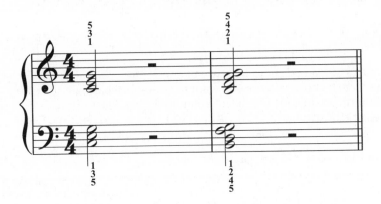

1. **With your hands held slightly above the notes in the chord, imagine the shape of the chord in your mind and feel (but don't play yet!) that shape in your fingers.**

2. **Allow your arm weight to drop onto the keyboard as you comfortably play the chord and hold the shape in your fingers.**

3. **With a loose, flexible feeling in your wrists, let the weight travel and be absorbed in your wrists with a light bounce.**

4. **Keeping the chord notes held down, let the wrist float back up and release the notes under your fingers as you lift up from the keyboard, releasing any muscle tension in your fingers, hands, arms, and shoulders.**

During the rest between the two chords, release any tension throughout your arms and torso, and prepare for the next chord shape as in Step 1.

A longer progression

Now try practicing the cycle in a longer progression. Don't hold any stiffness — after playing a chord, let your wrist relax and absorb the weight you've put into the keys. Instead of channeling the weight to your fingertips and holding it there as you press down the keys, let it travel to your wrists where the weight is absorbed and released with a slight bounce. You need to maintain just enough muscle tone and shape in your hands and fingers to hold down each chord note.

Finding the places to release muscle tension depends on the type of chordal passage you're playing. During a rest you have an obvious spot to relax your hands and release your muscles. On long-held chords you can release tension while holding down the notes, and you can find quick "breaths" as you release staccato chords. You'll have plenty of examples to practice these releases in the following exercises.

Voicing Chords

Every time you strike a chord you get to be a sound engineer — you can set your own EQ (or equalizer) levels with each chord. Maybe you want to hear more bass, more top note, or bring out the notes in the middle for the fullest sound possible. Most of the time you want the top note to sing out the strongest, with support from the bottom note next and the inner chord notes balanced next. When you play chords you continually fine-tune your voicing to highlight melodic movement that takes place within a chordal setting.

You can custom-balance each chord tone with subtle differences in your attack speed. You achieve this with variations in the quality of touch for each finger. The piano is designed to transmit and, in effect, amplify these nuances from the key to the hammer to the strings and into sound. Any number of variations in your touch affect the attack speed of each chord tone. Experiment with voicing in the next exercise, bringing out the moving voice, which changes from the top, to the middle, to the bottom note of the chord.

When you want to bring out a certain note within a chord, try using a gentle touch on the other chord notes. A gentle touch should slow the attack speed, bringing down their volume.

Chord Repetition

Tension and fatigue often come with playing passages of repeated chords. The challenge is to find a way to stay in a fluid cycle that allows some muscle release while keeping enough shape and tone to maintain a full, even sound.

Pulsing rhythms

This first exercise in repeated chords gives you practice with both short and long articulation. Keep your wrist high and loosely relaxed for the faster eighth-note chords, making room for a light bounce off the keyboard as you release the keys. Relax into the keys on the long quarter-note chords.

Changing dynamics

Now practice this same method while changing the dynamic range. Make sure you're playing all the chord notes when you play very softly — don't let your hands or fingers go slack. Increase the volume with a quicker attack speed rather than by hitting the keys harder.

Your fingers and wrist can move more quickly if they're not locked in tension. Keep enough tone in your wrist for the faster chord repetition, and then release any muscle tension on the long chords.

Simple Progressions, Adding Small Arm Motions

As you play chords in longer progressions, you'll get a better overall musical shape if you physically help shape the dynamics and phrasing. You can allow the melodic movement of the chords and the phrasing, indicated by the slur, to lead your hands and arms with a small, circular motion. Match your movement to the rhythmic motion and dynamic shape of the music.

Progression #1

Progression #2

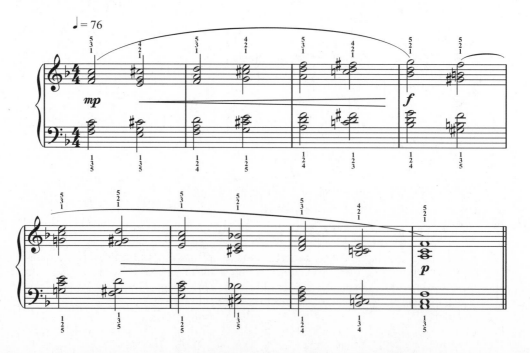

Chord and Melody Combination Exercises

The next exercises give you practice with some of the most common ways chords are combined with melody. Practice the cycle of tension and release with each exercise.

Chord and melody combo #1

The melody to the African American spiritual "Swing Low, Sweet Chariot" provides a nice setting for gospel-style chords. The hands trade off with the melody and three-part chordal background. Bring out the melody and balance the chords to shade its natural shape.

Chord and melody combo #2

The simple melody of the folk song "All the Pretty Little Horses" offers a good opportunity to practice constantly shifting harmonies. Practice balancing the softer left-hand chords under the melody, and use the rhythmic pattern in the left hand to practice your cycle of release.

Chord and melody combo #3

In the theme to the slow movement of Beethoven's seventh symphony, harmony and melody are equally important. Let both hands shape the dynamics and phrasing, and add to the melodic and harmonic movement of the theme.

Slowly

Performance Piece: "Battle Hymn of the Republic"

Bring a ringing, resonant sound to your performance by playing the chords with an even and quick attack. Coordinate your cycle of tension and release with the rhythmic pattern of the chords, making light wrist bounces on beats one and four of each measure.

Part III
Including Your Arms and Body

The 5th Wave — By Rich Tennant

"Normally, a cross hand technique is used for reaching upper register notes. But what you're doing is fine, as long as it doesn't hurt."

In this part . . .

You get more of your body in on the warm-up. You expand the movement of your hands and arms with scales of all kinds, up and down two octaves, hands-together, in parallel and contrary motion. Fingerings for every scale help make them easy to master. You bring your foot into the picture with pedaling exercises, and you get a total mind/body experience when you practice keyboard jumps both small and big, short and long.

Chapter 7

Extending Your Scales

. . . .

In This Chapter

▶ Practicing major, harmonic minor, and melodic minor scales

▶ Working on chromatic, diminished, and blues scales

▶ Establishing solid fingering for all scales

▶ Varying your practice methods for greater command

▶ Playing a performance piece to showcase your scales

. . . .

You've come to the chapter of scales, the heart of piano exercises. If you love them, you'll find lots to keep you happy here, and maybe some new scales to challenge your fingers. If you don't love them, well, hopefully you'll like them a little more after you try a few of them in a new presentation. You can make a selection of scales that fit your daily workout goals, or pick different scales on different days for variety.

In this chapter, you sharpen your crossover and pass-under skills as you extend single-note runs into two-octave scales with your hands together. If you need to review passing under and crossing over, see Chapter 4.

You can get a good workout here, with scales and fingering for all 12 major, harmonic minor, and melodic minor scales, plus diminished, chromatic, and blues scales. It's paradise if you seek speed and accuracy and if you love patterns. There's nothing like the feeling of flying up and down the keyboard as your scale-fingering starts clicking and you begin to feel a lightness in your touch.

How does scale practice connect with playing good music? Find out when you play the performance piece, one of Mozart's variations on the tune "Twinkle, Twinkle Little Star," at the end of the chapter.

The 12 Major, Harmonic Minor, and Melodic Minor Scales

The major and minor scales are the backbone of piano technique. And for good reason, because so much of the music we love is based on these scales. So these scales tend to loom large; many pianists even envision doom and horror at the thought of practicing scales up and down the keyboard for hours at a time. You can take a more practical, just-the-facts approach with the scales in this section.

Each scale is just two octaves up and down, and they're grouped so that you can play the major, harmonic minor, and melodic minor scales starting on the same note before moving on to the next key. You follow the circle of fifths, which adds one sharp to the key signature as you go from the key of C through the key of F♯, and then subtracts one flat from the key signature as you go from the key of D♭ through the key of F. Follow the fingerings carefully, and feel free to play them slowly or hands-alone as you get started.

C major, C harmonic minor, C melodic minor

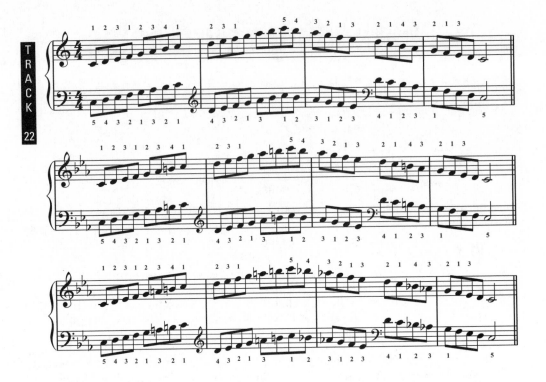

G major, G harmonic minor, G melodic minor

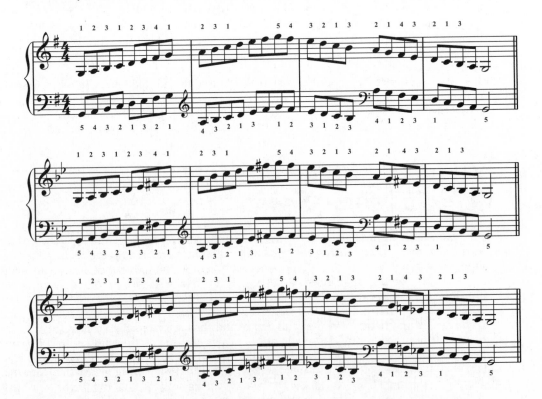

D major, D harmonic minor, D melodic minor

A major, A harmonic minor, A melodic minor

E major, E harmonic minor, E melodic minor

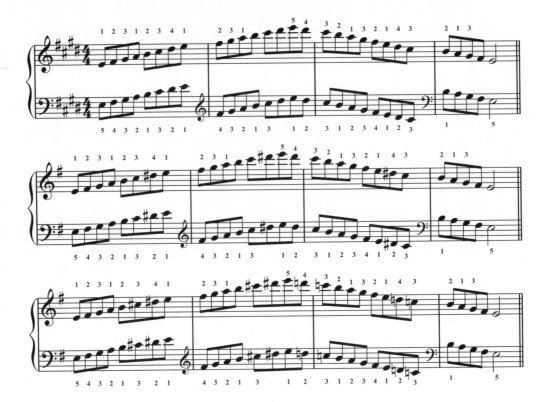

B major, B harmonic minor, B melodic minor

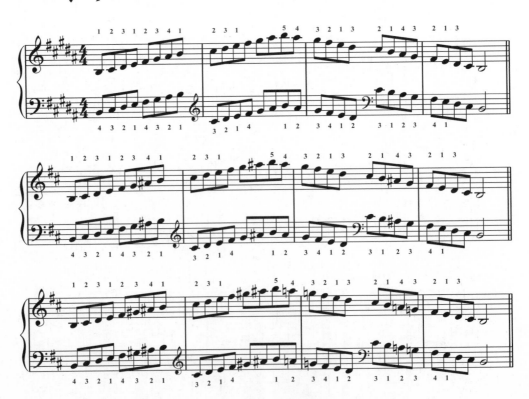

F♯ major, F♯ harmonic minor, F♯ melodic minor

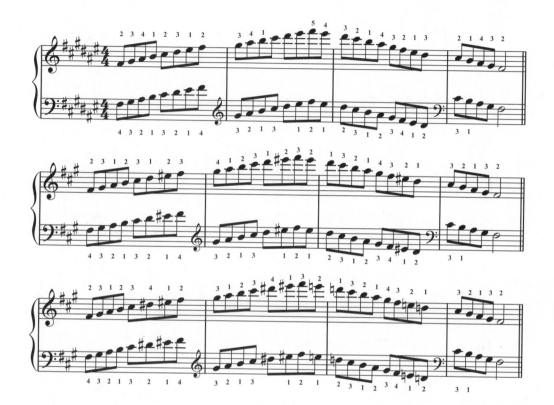

D♭ major, C♯ harmonic minor, C♯ melodic minor

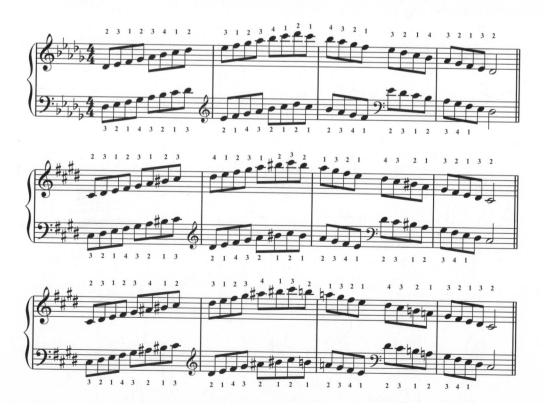

A♭ major, A♭ harmonic minor, A♭ melodic minor

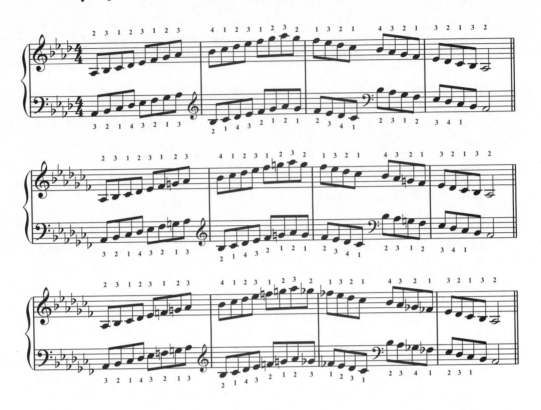

E♭ major, E♭ harmonic minor, E♭ melodic minor

B♭ major, B♭ harmonic minor, B♭ melodic minor

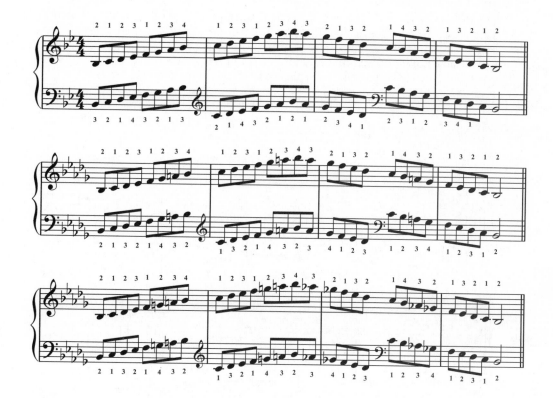

F major, F harmonic minor, F melodic minor

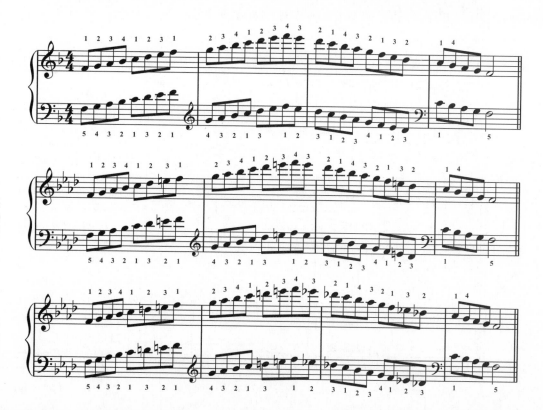

The Three Diminished Scales

The diminished, or octatonic, scale is unique and fun to practice because of its symmetrical pattern. The eight-note scale follows a whole-step/half-step/whole-step/half-step pattern, which means you can think of every other note as the root of a diminished scale consisting of the same eight notes. If that sounds confusing, just play one and you'll see. It also means you have only three diminished scales to learn. Here they are:

Starting on C

Starting on D♭

Starting on D

The Chromatic Scale

After you're comfortable with the fingering for the chromatic scale, try playing a two-octave scale starting on a different note, or in a different octave.

Play all the black keys with your third finger. Use your thumb to play all white keys except C and F in your right hand, and E and B in your left hand. Play these keys with your second finger.

Start on C for this exercise.

The 12 Blues Scales

The blues scale is a six-note scale made of the following scale tones: the root, flat third, fourth, sharp fourth (or flat fifth), fifth, and flat seventh of any given key.

Because of their unusual groups of intervals, blues scales are excellent for improving your crossover and pass-under technique.

C blues

G blues

D blues

A blues

E blues

B blues

F# blues

D♭ blues

A♭ blues

E♭ blues

B♭ blues

F blues

Gaining Greater Command of Scales

One of the best ways to practice scales is to vary the articulation and rhythm as you practice. You can gain greater command and improve finger flexibility with variations that take you out of the usual routine. Playing scales the same way, day after day, can get you practicing on autopilot, tuning out while your fingers go through the motions. To reinvigorate your scales, and reinforce fingering, change it up a bit by varying the articulation and rhythmic groupings. Stay with four-note patterns for all the scales so the pattern comes out evenly. Here are some suggested exercises — try some on your own, too.

Varied articulation

Varied rhythmic groupings

Performance Piece: Variation VII from "Variations on 'Twinkle, Twinkle, Little Star'"

This piece answers the question, "Why do I have to practice scales?!?" Mozart applied the fundamentals of music in undeniably musical ways, using them to give balance, character, and proportion to even the smallest of forms, like this variation.

W. A. Mozart

Chapter 8

Parallel and Contrary Motion

In This Chapter

▶ Exercising with hands in parallel and contrary motion

▶ Improving finger and hand independence

▶ Playing a performance piece with combined motion

Moving on from where the previous chapter left off, this chapter shows you how to continue practicing single-note lines in each hand, now with melodies that move in parallel and contrary motion. These exercises increase your hand and finger independence and improve your coordination.

The ultimate goal here is to integrate or combine multiple kinds of movement into one action. You may feel coordination-challenged when you try to rub your belly while patting your head, but that's mainly because you've never integrated the movements. Instead, imagine walking while turning your head to watch a car go by, or stirring a pot while talking on the phone. These actions are integrated, so you don't think about doing two things at once. The key to these parallel and contrary motion exercises is to integrate the multiple movements into a single feeling. You're teaching your body to feel a combination of movements as one, and adapting mentally to imagine the whole rather than all the parts.

Put it all together in the performance piece at the end of the chapter, a parallel/contrary motion jamboree on the folk tune "Turkey in the Straw."

Parallel Movement at the Octave

These exercises are similar to scales but with more melodic flexibility in the movement of the lines. Normal scale fingering applies most of the time, but the music takes you away from these patterns. The key to good fingering is finding the most comfortable solution to fit the music.

Parallel octave exercise #1

Parallel octave exercise #2

Parallel Movement at the Interval

Now your hands are moving on a parallel track, either a sixth or a tenth apart, instead of an octave apart. Try focusing on one hand at a time until you start to feel the integration kicking in. Even if you miss a few notes, focus your attention on one hand while the other rides along in parallel motion. Your goal is to visualize both hands moving together, the notes and movement clear in your mind's eye.

Parallel sixths

Parallel tenths

Contrary Motion Away from the Center

Contrary motion can be easier than parallel because the hands are playing symmetrical fingering patterns. Still, keeping your eyes up on the notes on the page can be a challenge. Develop a habit of reading the music bottom to top, your left hand before the right. Dare to keep your eyes on the music, visualize the synchronized movement, and trust your hands to find their place on the keyboard.

If sharing a key with both thumbs is awkward, let one rest on top of the other for the shared note.

Scalewise motion away from the center

Chromatic motion away from the center

TRACK 27

Contrary Motion Toward the Center

Check out my advice in the preceding section for tips on mastering these exercises.

Scalewise motion toward the center

Patterns toward the center

Combination Movement Exercise

Don't let the sixteenth notes scare you away from this exercise. It combines all the different types of movement covered in the chapter and provides a good fingering and coordination challenge. Make sure to look ahead to see what's coming in the next measure, and let 'er rip!

You'll be most successful if you can visualize all the moves before you play them. Your fingers don't know where to go until you direct them with a clear image of the moves they need to make.

Performance Piece: "Turkey in the Straw"

To capture the style of a fiddler's duet, the melody is paired with a parallel motion harmony part in the left hand. Try to match the articulation and dynamics in both hands to help bring off the effect.

Chapter 9

Footwork: Using the Damper Pedal

In This Chapter

▶ Reviewing the basics of pedaling

▶ Practicing pedaling with chords and melody lines

▶ Enhancing your playing with fancy pedaling

▶ Performance piece: "Simple Gifts," featuring you, your fingers, and your foot

This chapter is all about your right foot, and what it can do together with your hands to make your music more musical. I tell you how to use the sustain pedal to get a range of different sounds, blend tones, and bring off tricks that you can't do without it.

The piano is essentially a percussion instrument, meaning that it produces a pitch that has a quick attack when you strike a key and the hammer strikes the strings. If you hold this key down, the pitch has a slow decay, because you're keeping the damper inside the piano off the string, allowing it to vibrate freely. But after you release the key, the damper returns to stop the string from vibrating, stopping the sound. Sustaining the sound is possible with the sustain pedal, which keeps the damper off the strings for you.

By using the pedal in a careful way, you gain a greater range of expression. It can help you to "sing" a melody, connect music in phrases, and create greater resonance and atmospheric illusions. Overuse of the pedal can have some big drawbacks — unintentional mixing of harmonies, blurring notes, and obscuring any articulation that should be clear. Your careful and attentive listening helps avoid these problems.

This chapter gives you practice pedaling for a variety of purposes and helps you avoid overusing the pedal. You can show off your pedaling technique with an arrangement of the Shaker melody "Simple Gifts," the performance piece at the end of the chapter.

Pedaling Chords

The two most common pedaling indications are shown in the following figure. Press the pedal down at the "Ped." sign, and release (pedal up) at the asterisk or at the bracket ending the line. These indications are always shown below the bass staff.

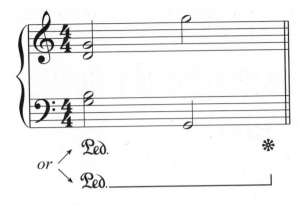

The notch in the line in the following figure indicates where to change the pedal, quickly clearing any sustained sound (pedal up) and resetting the sustain (pedal down). Changing the pedal requires careful attention to clearing the harmony cleanly and completely.

Good pedaling is all a matter of timing and listening. Your goal is to train your ear to listen for a smooth transition and a clean change from note to note and chord to chord. You don't want to time your pedaling to match your hands, releasing and then pressing the pedal down as your fingers move from one chord to another; if you do, you'll hear a gap between chords. This is because you're lifting both the keys and the pedal together, so the dampers stop the sound when your fingers leave the keys. You need the sustain pedal down at this time. You have to wait to change the pedal so it happens simultaneously with playing the next chord, with only enough overlap to create a smooth connection between chords and a clean resetting of the pedal. You want a seamless transition — no gap — as if you were simply singing one note to another. After you change the pedal and the previous chord clears, you can release the keys and let the pedal do its job.

Check out the way your foot is positioned. Your heel should stay on the floor, and your toes can rest on the pedal. Some pedals require more weight and pressure, and foot size and power are all different. You can use your longer toes plus some of the ball of your foot to press down the pedal, but as always go for comfort and ease. Your ankle is the hinge that allows your foot to move with the least amount of movement and effort.

TIP

Pedaling shouldn't affect your general posture, so if you find that you have to shift around or adjust your balance to accommodate pedaling, you may not have started from a good position. See Chapter 1 for more on posture.

The first two exercises use the same chord progression to practice the pedaling basics.

Broken-chord pedaling

In this exercise, you change pedal on a single note.

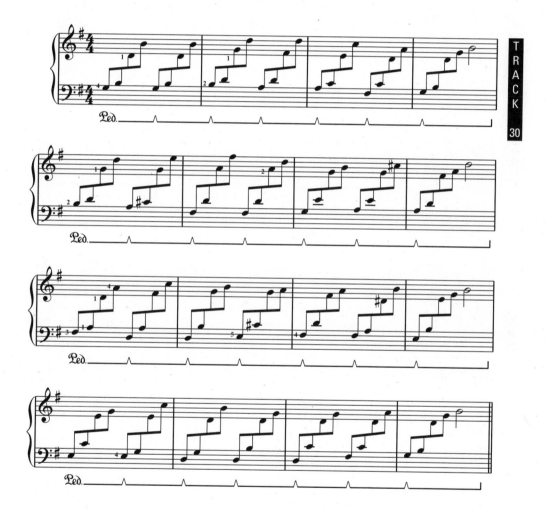

Block-chord pedaling

In this exercise you change going from chord to chord and on any moving lines within the harmony. Listen for those smooth transitions!

Pedaling Changes on a Single Line

Although changing the pedal with the change of harmony is a general rule, you'll want to change it more frequently when you're also playing a melodic line.

Uniform pedal changes

When you have a slow, meandering melody, you may change the pedal before the harmony changes so the melody doesn't get too blurry. Try it with this bluesy melody.

Varied pedal changes

You can enhance your legato phrasing by pedaling even more frequently along the melodic line. This is especially useful in melodic lines with a wide range that call for a singer's phrasing. The pedal can smooth over wide jumps and the places you have to lift your hand to change position. Try it with the melody to Stephen Foster's "Jeanie with the Light Brown Hair."

Pedaling for Effect

Use the sustain pedal for *atmospheric effect* (sustaining notes in a line for a blurred effect) or to help sustain a note or chord over several measures.

Blurred lines and long sustains

In this exercise, the pedal helps sustain the long notes in one hand while smoothing the melodic movement in the other hand. Combined with a soft dynamic, this technique helps create a misty, mysterious effect.

Sustaining as the hands leave the keyboard

You can use the pedal to give notes their full value when you have to move your hands to a new position on the keyboard. This can also be a plus musically, because you can exaggerate the rhythms and the differences between the long and short articulations.

Performance Piece: "Simple Gifts"

The pedal helps give a bell-like quality to the half-note octaves in the right hand at the beginning and in the left hand from the middle to the end of this performance piece. Notice how the pedal is up when the melody is in the left hand, where it may muddy the line, and down when the melody is in the upper register of the right hand, where the mild blurring adds a nice effect. During the last three measures, you keep the pedal down to layer the G-major chord over the full range of the piano.

Chapter 10

Jumping Across the Keyboard

. . . .

In This Chapter

▶ Jumping from note to note and chord to chord

▶ Discovering new accuracy skills

▶ Exercising with left-hand accompaniment patterns

▶ Playing a ragtime-style performance piece featuring hand jumps

. . . .

Covering the full territory of the 88 keys is certainly one of the enticing attributes of the piano. Jumping registers, from low to high or high to low, is a potent tool that few other instruments can match. The exercises in this chapter give you practice jumping from one note to another and from chord to chord, over both smaller and larger intervals. This practice will help your accuracy as you move across the keyboard, help develop your "feel" for where your hands go, and improve your sense of distance as your hands work from small jumps over shorter intervals to big jumps over three octaves.

This chapter also gives you lots of practice with the most common left-hand patterns — a variety of bass-note-to-chord accompaniments essential to playing waltzes, rags, marches, and many other dance rhythms.

The exercises warm you up for the lively performance piece at the end of the chapter. The piece is a ragtime-style number that keeps both hands jumping.

Jumping and Landing Accuracy Skills

The key to making good, accurate jumps is the same whether the jump is big or small: Maintain a comfortable, balanced hand position as you jump from the starting hand position across the keyboard to your landing destination. Jumping with an overextended pinky and your hand outstretched like the descent of a giant hawk upon its prey is very common. Instead, the image you want to keep in mind is of a frog jumping from lily pad to lily pad. Though a frog may extend its legs to jump high in the air (you don't need to do that part), it starts and lands with its body centered over the lily pad, contracting to the same closed, restful shape. Your hands are two frogs. As they jump from one position to another, they should look the same before and after the jump. You can practice this skill with every exercise.

Note-to-note jumps

In this first exercise, you simply try jumping from note to note.

Visualize each jump before you make the move. Include the relaxed, frog-like shape of your hand, the arc it traces as it jumps, and the specific finger landing on its target key.

Note-to-chord jumps

Same principle — visualize and jump to an easy, relaxed position on the chord notes, and don't overextend your fingers or move with your hand stuck in an awkward hand position.

Chord-to-chord jumps

Make sure your forearms aren't overly tense and contracted; you want just enough muscle flexion to keep your position stable. Your hands should also have enough flexion to hold their position as they come down into the keys without collapsing in the joints. Allow some flexibility in your wrists to absorb the weight as you play the chords. (See Chapter 6 for more on playing chords.)

Mastering More Complicated Jumps

The next two exercises increase the challenge level with greater hand independence, varied articulation, and faster hand position changes.

Accents on the downbeat

Here, your frogs get a springboard from the upbeat (on beat four) to the downbeat (on beat one). Practice with a light upbeat and a well-accented downbeat.

Accents on the upbeat

Now move the accent to the upbeat, with a light, springy downbeat.

Jumping with Both Hands Together

After you practice jumps with one hand, you can synchronize jumps in both hands — first matching movements in parallel motion and then mirroring the jumps in contrary motion. Take your time, and make sure you're playing all the notes with an equally solid touch.

Two-hand parallel motion jumps

Two-hand contrary motion jumps

Left-Hand Accompaniment Patterns (With Pedal)

Jumps are an especially common feature of left-hand accompaniments. Setting a steady rhythm and laying down the harmonic foundation are often the jobs of your left hand, while your right hand handles the melodic duties. You can exercise this vital function in the next four exercises. First, try it with the help of the sustain pedal for smoother accompaniment patterns.

Bass-note-to-chord pattern in 4/4

You'll find this left-hand pattern when you play marches and dance rhythms like the foxtrot. Lifting the pedal on the upbeats makes the rhythm distinctive.

Bass-note-to-chord pattern in 3/4

This is a common pattern for a slow waltz, like Satie's well-known Gymnopédies. You get a full harmonic sound as well as a smooth jump with the pedal down for each measure.

Left-Hand Accompaniment Patterns (Without Pedal)

Without the sustain pedal, your left-hand part is more exposed. So practicing without the pedal is good for keeping an even rhythm, matching articulation, and smooth movement. If you hesitate, lurch to a chord, or miss a bass note, you'll hear it!

Ragtime and stride pattern

Here's an accompaniment pattern typical of a ragtime or basic stride piano style.

 Moving quickly off the bass note and rushing up to the chord is tempting, but this action usually cuts the bass note short. Stay on the bass note a little longer than you think you should to give the rhythm and harmony a solid foundation.

Waltz pattern

Let your right hand sing out the melody while the left hand accompanies it with a waltz pattern.

Performance Piece: "Lily Pad Rag"

The unique combination of a syncopated right-hand melody set over a steady 4-beat left-hand pattern gives ragtime its bouncy allure. As you work on "Lily Pad Rag," develop a clear mental picture of when and where a melody note coincides with the left hand and when it is played between beats and held over, at the syncopation. Give extra emphasis to these syncopated notes.

Part IV
Integration and Independence

The 5th Wave   By Rich Tennant

Okay, this time try not to take such a deep breath.

In this part . . .

You put it all together with fun and flair. If you're look-ing for greater challenges, you can find them in this part. And even if you're not there's plenty to gain what-ever your level.

You integrate many of the moves presented in previous sections, putting them together in a variety of melodic and harmonic settings. You practice arpeggio and octave exer-cises and independent hand moves like passing a melody from hand to hand, crossing a hand over a hand, and play-ing at the extreme registers of the keyboard. You practice chord progressions and cadences in Chapter 14, and ornaments in Chapter 15, with examples and explanations that make it fun and easy. Chapter 16 is filled with rhythm exercises that challenge you to stay mentally ahead of your hands so you can conduct and coordinate all your moves.

Chapter 11

Playing Arpeggios

· ·

In This Chapter

▶ Improving finger accuracy and independence in open hand positions

▶ Practicing three- and four-note chord arpeggios

▶ Exercising practical broken-chord patterns

▶ "Harp Heaven": A performance piece filled with arpeggios

· ·

*P*laying broken-chord patterns, or *arpeggios,* on the piano is very satisfying. In addition to the beauty and speed they can give your playing, they lend a bit of the style from the guitar and harp. These string instruments play broken chords and arpeggios naturally as their strings are strummed and swept. In fact, "arpeggio" comes from the Italian word for harp, *arpa.*

When you play the notes of a chord individually, you're playing a broken chord, or arpeggio.

Practicing arpeggio patterns is excellent for improving several different technical areas:

✔ Your accuracy making short interval jumps from finger to finger

✔ Your crossover and pass-under technique as you practice multi-octave arpeggios

✔ Your finger control and independence with a mix of arpeggio patterns

Now that you're itching to get going, on to the exercises. When you get to the end of the chapter, you can display your dazzling speed in the arpeggio-driven performance piece, "Harp Heaven."

Finger Jumps

In this section, you make a sequence of interval jumps from finger to finger. Your hand shape is open, with a wider span compared to five-finger position. The interval jumps are the same moves you make when you play arpeggios, but the exercises give you practice with each interval separately, starting with thirds and then on to fourths and fifths.

The fingerings in each exercise will guide your hand position changes, so take some time to map out the hand positions as you go through them.

Jumping thirds

Jumping fourths

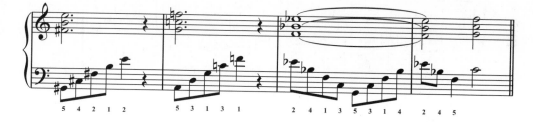

Jumping fifths

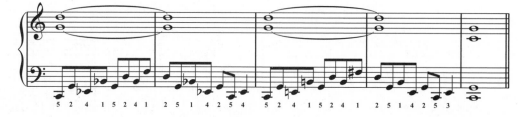

The Arpeggiator

The exercises in this section give you a workout with arpeggios on major, minor, diminished, and seventh chords. You get simple up-down patterns as well as nonsequential and inverted chord patterns.

Practice hands-alone to really focus on the individual arpeggios. For a challenge, practice these arpeggios with both staccato and legato articulation.

Triad arpeggio exercise #1

Triad arpeggio exercise #2

Seventh-chord arpeggio exercise

Broken Chords (And How to Fix Them)

Broken-chord patterns are so common in accompaniment figures that you rarely notice they're simple arpeggios. This section gives you four patterns that are found in a wide range of styles.

Alberti bass exercise

The Alberti bass, named after the 18th-century Italian composer Domenico Alberti, is common in classical-style accompaniments. You'll find it in all kinds of piano music by Mozart, Haydn, and Beethoven. The pattern is a simple re-ordering of the chord notes in an arpeggio. This next piece, adapted from Karl Czerny's setting of a Scotch Air, features the Alberti bass throughout the left-hand part. You might find it natural, and indeed comfortable, to rotate your forearm gently from the outside (pinky-side) to the inside (thumb side) as you play this pattern.

Guitar-style broken chord exercise

Playing guitar-style arpeggio patterns often involves spreading the chord out over both hands to capture the wide range common in guitar chord voicing. The next song is a folk-style arrangement of the classic "Careless Love," with the right hand in a dual role playing the melody and completing the arpeggio pattern started in the left hand.

Moderately

Blues-style broken chord exercise

Although you'll easily recognize the blues pattern in this piece, it's fun to realize it's simply an arpeggio set in a triplet rhythm. Try the pattern with the melody to W.C. Handy's "St. Louis Blues."

Octave and extended broken chord exercise

For a big, full piano sound, you can extend the arpeggio up to the octave and beyond in your accompaniment. The following extended pattern is a great exercise for the left hand. Try to keep the arpeggio smooth and even as you manage the crossovers and pass-unders in this version of "House of the Rising Sun."

Try the alternate fingerings (in parentheses) to see if the hand positions are more comfortable for your hand.

Performance Piece: "Harp Heaven"

You'll be able to play these arpeggios both fast and lightly if you anticipate the change in harmony from measure to measure. Get the feel of the chord progression by practicing each chord shape in both your hands before you play.

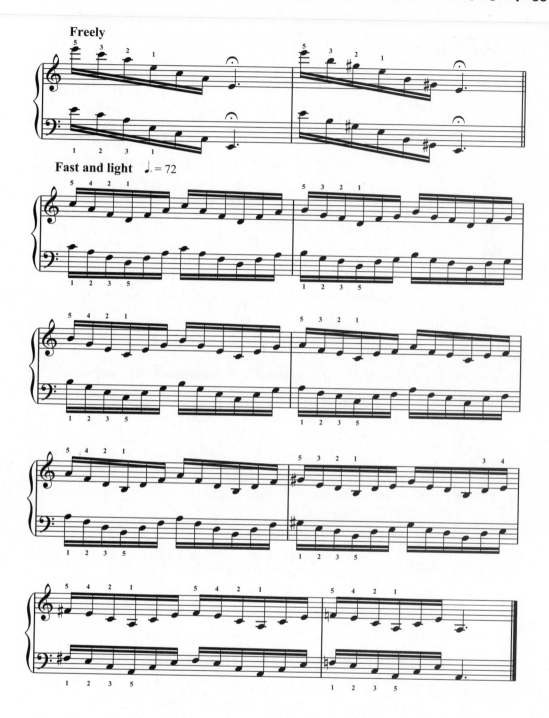

Chapter 12

Alternating Hands

· ·

In This Chapter

▶ Trying fancy moves across the keyboard

▶ Making use of hand-to-hand scales and arpeggios

▶ Crossing hands

▶ Attempting strange and extreme keyboard positions

· ·

The alternating-hand techniques covered in this chapter are not only fun to play, but also useful in all kinds of keyboard music, from Scarlatti to Ravel, Blues to Broadway, Liszt to Liberace. Pianists typically love to show off, and what better way than an impressive display of handoffs and crossovers?

A handoff is achieved by passing a melodic line from one hand to the other. Typically your left hand will hand off an ascending line to your right hand, and vice versa.

A hand crossover, not to be confused with a finger crossover (see Chapter 4), is employed when you find it handy (and impressive) to cross one hand over the other to grab a note or a chord or two.

Even if showing off isn't your thing, the exercises here help bring both hands to an equal level, because they're collaborating on the main musical part instead of one supporting the other.

Hand-to-Hand Scale Handoffs

As you hand off the scale from hand to hand, you want a smooth transition. Try to fool your ears; the handoff should be so smooth that you can't tell where one hand takes over from the other. And you should hear no noticeable change in dynamic or articulation.

Some of these techniques look complicated written on the grand staff! Unless marked with a "R.H." or "L.H." your right hand will play the notes on the top staff and your left hand will play the notes on the bottom staff.

Scale handoff exercise #1

Prepare the hand position for both hands before you begin each phrase. Playing a smooth scale in one hand is easier if the other hand is waiting quietly in position to take over.

Scale handoff exercise #2

Hand-to-Hand Arpeggio Handoffs

The same hand preparation from the previous section applies to the chord arpeggios: If you anticipate your hand positions before you move, your arpeggios will sound much better.

Aim for a smooth line throughout the arpeggio. Just like the exercises in legato phrasing, a bit of an overlap can really help connect the notes and bridge any gaps. (See Chapter 3 for more on legato phrasing.)

Arpeggio handoff exercise #1

Arpeggio handoff exercise #2

Crossing Over

As you incorporate more and more of your body, remember to check your posture and comfort at the keyboard. In these exercises, give yourself room for both hands to cross over comfortably, with enough distance between you and the keyboard so you're not squeezed in.

You may have to adjust the height of each wrist, with a high arch in the crossing hand and a lower wrist position for the hand underneath.

Crossing over with the right hand

Crossing over with the left hand

One Hand on Top

The next two exercises give you some practice with top/bottom hand positions. They're fun and provide a visual treat, yet they can be tricky and challenge your hand independence.

Your hands should be in a nestled position, with some air space in between to allow independent movement. Play these gently, with a lightly rocking rhythm.

Right hand on top exercise

Left hand on top exercise

Extreme Keyboard Positions

When you're moving to and from these extreme registers, you have a lot more movement to coordinate. Keep in mind that your weight support should come from your lower body — your sitting bones and legs — leaving your arms and hands free to move. Be aware of the weight shifting when you move left and right, and use the exercise to examine whether you're shifting your weight easily and smoothly from your left-side sitting bone and leg to your right-side sitting bone and leg.

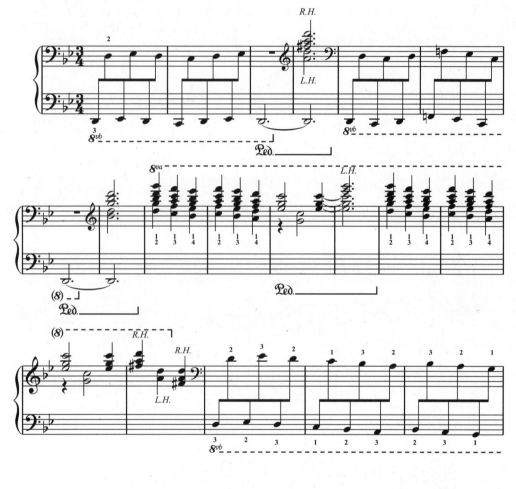

Full Keyboard Exercises

These exercises move over four and five octaves, working with triad arpeggios, block-chord triads, and an exercise with seventh chords in arpeggio and block-chord combinations. Start off slowly and increase your speed as you improve.

Full keyboard arpeggios

Try this exercise "air piano" style: Practice your hand movements on this exercise with your hands touching, but not playing, the keys. You'll usually find where you're over- or undershooting your movement.

Full keyboard triads

Full keyboard seventh chords

Chord "Drumming"

A good approach to chord drumming is to tap the rhythms (gently) on the closed piano lid until you develop an easy, rhythmic groove. Or be creative and use a different surface: Drum on your lap, two pots turned upside down like bongos, or even the tense muscles of someone's back. Try this exercise with hands in motion.

TRACK 44

Performance Piece: "El Choclo"

This popular tango by Angel Villoldo allows you to show off your panoply of moves — hand drumming, handoffs, and crossovers.

Chapter 13

Stretching Out with Octaves and Broken Octaves

Yes, octaves are hard. They're hard for everybody, and to a certain extent everybody has to figure out how their own unique hands best meet the challenge. But give this chapter a try; you'll find some new exercises designed to help you examine and improve your octave technique, and you may also find some tips here to make playing octaves easier.

Octave practice is similar to chord playing (see Chapter 6) because you use your entire hand as a single unit, in contrast to finger independence exercises. Good octave technique combines an open (but not overextended) hand position with a confident, comfortable arm drop. Most of your attention is focused on the position of your pinky and thumb, the fingers that do most of the note playing. But you also look at how the rest of your hand helps out. The height of your wrist, the angle of the inside fingers, and your depth into the keyboard are all factors in improving octave technique. As you go through the exercises in this chapter, you apply octave position to scales, jumps, broken octaves, and chords.

Because every hand is a different size and shape, you need to be on the lookout for tension and overstretching. Take breaks to relieve tightness and fatigue.

Opening Up to the Octave

There is no single, best way for you to play octaves; what works for one can be different for others and is based on the size and shape of your hands and fingers. So the best way to start is to observe your hand and fingers while playing octaves. Examine the movement of your hand, the overall hand shape, the position of your fingers playing the octaves, and the position of the fingers that aren't playing any keys. If you have small hands, you may not be able to play octaves from a high arch position of the wrist. If you have long fingers, you may need to keep your second, third, and fourth fingers relatively straight so they don't get in the way. Closely examine the thumb and pinky joints to see whether they are collapsed or whether you can modify their angle for more control. Look to maximize your advantages and minimize your disadvantages.

Octave scale exercise

This exercise begins with your hand in an easy, open fifth position. As you expand the intervals out to a sixth, seventh, and then to the octave, maintain a consistent shape, control, and touch. In other words, copy the feeling (firm in the pinky and thumb joints, more relaxed and rounded in the rest of the hand) as you expand the interval out to the octave. Try playing toward the outside edge of the keyboard; you may find it easier on white-key passages like this.

Octave interval exercise

For this exercise, try to keep the octave shape as you move across the keyboard over a variety of close intervals. Keep the open shape, but don't tense your muscles into a locked grip.

If your hands are big enough, use your fourth finger on the upper note to facilitate passages. This position creates smoother horizontal movement, especially with the fourth finger on a black key.

Octave Jumps

For octave jumps, develop a light bouncing action, using the release of the keys as a cue to release tension in your hand. Here are some tips to keep in mind:

✔ Focus on your fifth finger — that's where most of the misses happen. You'll need a bit more firmness in your pinky, with the thumb more relaxed and not grabbing.

✔ When you land into the octaves, aim down into the keys, pointing with your first and fifth fingers. This requires opening your hand into a bigger arch for accuracy.

✔ If your wrist drops down after you play the octave, make sure it returns to a nice high position while your fingers hold down the notes.

Don't worry about playing wrong notes. Your main goals are developing a clear mental image of where and how you're moving and practicing a comfortable, confident hand move. You'll play more right notes as you realize these goals.

Exercise with shorter jumps

Exercise with longer jumps

Broken Octaves

Give your hands a bit of a break by alternating the octave practicing with some broken octaves. First, prepare your hand in a comfortable, open octave position over both notes.

Exercise with wrist rotation

Using a gentle wrist rotation and transferring weight from your pinky to your thumb, and thumb to pinky, you can provide a tension-relief rhythm in your hand.

Exercise with hand contraction and expansion

Now exaggerate the weight transfer when you cross your second finger over your first, focusing on a firm attack with your second finger. Allow your fifth finger to leave its note during this move. Your hand contracts to cross over, and expands back out to the octave position.

Octave Chords

As you add inner notes to the octave, you want to observe your hands again. Make sure that your knuckles aren't collapsed and that your wrist isn't stuck in an extreme angle — either too high or too low. Go for an even, comfortable position and a fluid movement playing these octave chords. You want to feel your fingertips reach into the keys, so keep an active connection with your fingertips as you move your hand from position to position. It's a tricky combination you're after: overall, a firm hand shape, but not so locked in a grip that you prevent the supple movement of individual parts.

Adding one inner note

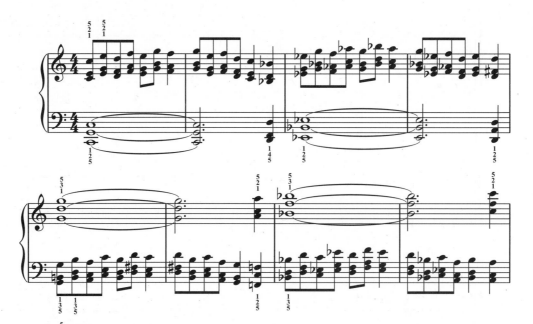

Adding two inner notes

Performance Piece: "Schumann's Octave Workout"

This piece is an adaptation of the first dance piece from Robert Schumann's "Papillons." It's an excellent workout for right-hand octaves.

Chapter 14

Chord Progressions and Cadences

· ·

In This Chapter

▶ Trying triad and seventh chord patterns

▶ Checking out chord cadences, turnarounds, and sequences

▶ Carrying out chord progression exercises

▶ Performance piece: A four-part Bach chorale

· ·

The fun and fascination of playing chord progressions comes in exploring their dual vertical and horizontal function. The vertical role is in each chord itself — how it's constructed from bottom to top. The horizontal role is in the way chords progress from one to another; how every good progression is a unique flow of harmonies.

The movement of chords is similar to the movement of voices in vocal music like chorales and hymns. A typical four-part chorale is divided into parts for the four different vocal ranges: soprano, alto, tenor, and bass. While each part sings its own melody line, harmonic movement is created when the parts are combined. And, generally speaking, the smoother the melodic movement of each part, the smoother the harmonic movement will be. This applies to playing chord progressions on the piano, too.

Getting some practice with chord progressions allows you to improve your facility with chords and to focus on balancing the horizontal movement of each chord note with the vertical structure of each chord.

The best thing about practicing chord progressions is developing the ability to recognize the chords you're playing and their function within the musical phrase. This recognition of chord function can improve your interpretation of the music you play because harmonic function is fundamental to expressing a musical idea. And after chord sequences, cadences, and other patterns become familiar to you, they'll become easier to play.

Triad Progressions

These exercises work with three-note chords in both hands, getting your fingers nimble and giving your eyes and ears practice recognizing common chord movement.

Diatonic triad progressions

First practice some progressions using triads built on the diatonic scale, and their inversions. Building chords on each note of the diatonic scale makes three types of triad: major, minor, and diminished.

These C-major diatonic triads move scale-wise, keeping two, and then one common chord tone with each change of chord. Practice hands-alone if playing the chords in both hands is difficult.

The alternate fingerings (in parentheses) might be a better fit for your hands. Try them, and feel free to use them in the following exercises.

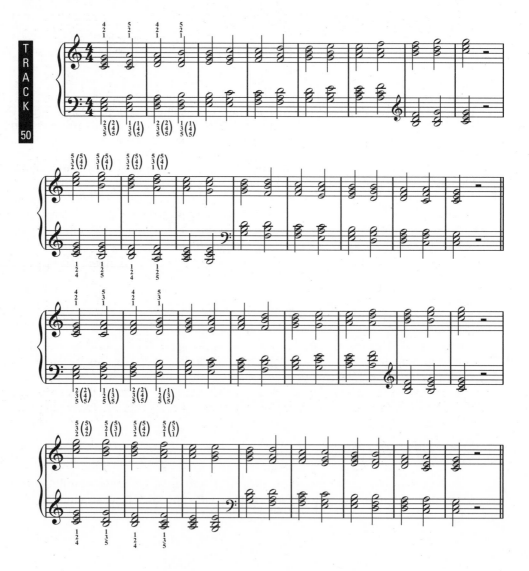

Chromatic triad progressions

Next you can include *nondiatonic triads* (triads with notes outside the diatonic scale) and then triads built on the A harmonic minor scale. This exercise has a greater variety of triads: major, minor, diminished, augmented, and suspended. Maneuvering through a more chromatic progression is more of a challenge.

Seventh Chord Progressions

Chords can have many functions, but the standout function of a dominant seventh chord is leading to a harmonic resolution on a major or minor triad. This function is easy to hear, because in the context of a progression, the tension caused by the notes in a dominant seventh chord tells you that the chord is, to put it simply, unresolved.

In these next two exercises you get some chord-resolution practice with dominant seventh and minor seventh chords.

Seventh chord progressions exercise #1

This exercise has dominant sevenths that resolve to the six major and minor triads in the diatonic scale: the I, ii, iii, IV, V, and vi chords.

If you like repeating a sequence exercise like this one over and over, watch that you don't tune out and let your fingers go on autopilot. To keep your mind engaged, play the eight-measure phrases in a random order to keep your thinking ahead of your playing.

Seventh chord progressions exercise #2

In the first half of this exercise, you cycle through all 12 dominant seventh chords by playing around the circle of fifths (see the Cheat Sheet and Chapter 7 for more on the circle of fifths). On the second half of the exercise, the chord sequence has minor seventh chords leading to dominant seventh chords in a descending pattern.

Chord Cadences and Familiar Patterns

This section shows you some chord patterns you find frequently in all types of music: cadences, turnarounds, and sequences.

Cadences

A *cadence* — when a chord progression comes to a close — is a short progression, usually two or three chords, which establishes the tonality and communicates a strong sense of resolution. Here are a variety of common cadences in C major and A minor.

Turnarounds and sequences

Turnarounds get you, harmonically speaking, turned around so that you can go back to the home key. This usually means getting to the V chord, by any number of means, which will lead you back home to the I chord.

Chord sequences, a repeating pattern of chord changes, are a fundamental building block of chord progressions. Practice to get your fingers familiar with these patterns.

Extended Chord Progressions

Here are two short pieces where the chord progressions are the defining feature of the composition. The first is in major key, the second in minor. Both extended progressions use diatonic chords, nondiatonic chords, sequences, and cadences.

Extended major-key chord progression

This exercise is adapted from Tchaikovsky's *Morning Prayer,* Album for the Young, Opus 39.

Extended minor-key chord progression

This exercise is adapted from Chopin's *Prelude,* Opus 28, No. 20.

Chords in One Hand, Melody in the Other

In the next two exercises, the chord progression takes a back-seat role to the melodic pattern. Yet recognizing the structure that the progression gives to the music can have a positive influence on the way you play. Both of these chord progressions will be familiar to you, but the melody is replaced by a melodic exercise. See whether you recognize the songs by just their chord progressions.

Chords with melody exercise #1

This chord progression in the right hand is from "We Wish You A Merry Christmas," with a melodic pattern in the left hand.

Chords with melody exercise #2

While you're in the holiday spirit, see whether you recognize the chord progression to "Auld Lang Syne." Here the right hand has the melodic pattern and the left hand has the chords.

Performance Piece: "Awake, My Heart, and Sing"

In Bach's chorale 93, "Awake, My Heart, and Sing" (adapted from *371 Harmonized Chorales and 69 Chorale Melodies,* by Johann Sebastian Bach), you find a perfect balance of the melodic (horizontal) and the harmonic (vertical). You get to take a two-handed shot at playing some four-part harmony.

Chapter 15

Trilling Thrills and Other Fancy Ornaments

. . . .

In This Chapter

▶ Playing ornaments: Grace notes, trills, mordents, and turns

▶ Other fancy embellishments: Repeated note, rolled chord, glissando, and tremolo exercises

▶ Performance piece: An ornament-filled aria from *Rigoletto*

. . . .

*O*rnaments are for decoration, and because of their role as embellishment, they're more like the icing on the cake of music rather than the cake itself. Or they're the cornice on the façade of a building rather than its foundation. But wherever you hear music, there they are: adorning the flute and fiddle melodies in folk music, adding deeper color to the blues, embellishing the delicate harpsichord sonatas of the baroque era, and giving sopranos something to trill about at the opera. So they must be important.

But even if they're essential, all the funny signs, abbreviations, and shrunken notes can be intimidating. There's nothing like the feeling that you're playing something the wrong way, with the ornament police waiting in the wings to cart you away for mordent offenses.

This chapter covers the most common ornaments, how they're written, and how they're played. You'll play exercises for each ornament so they'll be fresh in both your fingers and mind. The performance piece at the end of the chapter combines these decorative techniques in a highly embellished version of an aria from Verdi's opera, *Rigoletto*.

Grace Notes

Grace notes are a type of musical ornament written with small, "cue-size" notes. Here are three facts to remember about grace notes:

✔ Grace notes can lead stepwise up or down to the next note, jump up or down to another note, or appear in a group of two or more grace notes.

✔ They have no time value, so instead of counting them as you count other note values, you play them quickly (but not hurriedly) before the main note, which you give its full time value.

✔ Unless they're accented, you should play them lightly and without emphasis.

Trills

A trill can start on the written note and alternate with its upper neighbor, or it can start on the upper neighbor and alternate with the written note. It was more common to start on the upper neighbor in music of the Baroque and Classical eras (Bach, Mozart, and Haydn, for example). You can practice the trills in this exercise either way or both ways, if you like. Gaining control of the trilling fingers is the object, so in this exercise you alternate the trilling notes in a slower rhythm and speed up to the trill playing faster rhythms.

A common misconception is that all ornaments have to be played very fast. In fact, matching the ornaments with the character and tempo of the music is a better way to go.

Mordents

A simple and delicate three-note decoration, a mordent evokes the style of baroque keyboard music. The two types of mordent are upper and lower. An upper mordent sign above a note tells you to ornament it by playing that note, and then its upper neighbor, and back to the main note in quick succession. When you see a lower mordent, which has the vertical line through the sign, above a note, ornament it by playing that note, and then its lower neighbor, and back to the main note in quick succession. In this exercise, a brief minuet by Haydn, the small staff shows you how to play each mordent.

If you see an accidental above or below an ornament sign, it applies to the neighboring note in the ornament rather than the main note.

Turns

You see the sign indicating a turn placed between two notes or over a note. Either way, it signals a four-note ornament starting on the upper neighbor, moving to the written note, and then to the lower neighbor, and back to the main note. The small staff in the next exercise shows you how to play the turns.

Repeated Notes

Rapid, repeated notes capture the spirit of guitar tremolos, trumpet fanfares, and especially drum rolls and other percussive effects.

Repeated notes are best played with two or more fingers in succession. The faster you want to play them, the more you need to switch fingers. After you get the hang of it, it's much easier and the results are more effective. If you try a variety of finger combinations, you may find a new move that works best for you. Start by comparing the alternate fingerings shown in the first three measures.

Repeated notes in triplet rhythms

Repeated notes in eighth- and sixteenth-note rhythms

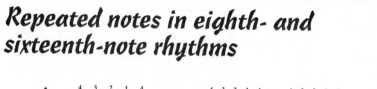

R-R-R-Rolling Chords

The squiggly line to the left of a chord means to roll the chord, the notes sounding pyramid-style, by playing each chord tone, individually and rapidly, from the lowest to the highest note, holding down each chord tone so that all the notes sound together when you get to the top note. Stay loose and flexible in your fingers and practice the subtle rotation from the left side of your hand to the right.

Rolling chords in the right hand

Time the roll so the top note of the right-hand chord is played on the beat, simultaneously with the bass note in the left hand.

Rolling chords in both hands

Roll from bottom to top, starting with the left hand and ending with the top note of the right hand on the beat.

The Glissando

Whether you're of the Jerry Lee Lewis, the Liberace, or the Chico Marx school of glissando, finding an easy way to "gliss" depends on two things:

✔ Finding the right angle to hold your finger(s) to move comfortably up or down the keyboard and still make the keys go down fast enough to produce sound.

✔ Making contact with the keys at the side edge of the keytop rather than at the wooden side of the key, which might stop you (painfully) in your tracks.

For a glissando from the center of the keyboard going out with either hand, I recommend using the nails of the third and fourth fingers, paired close together and facing the direction they're going, with your fingers curved to allow your wrist to stay flat.

For a glissando going into the center of the keyboard with either hand, I recommend using your thumb nail, again positioned so the nail faces the direction it's moving, and keeping the rest of your hand shape as close to normal as possible, ready to resume the old (ho-hum) fingers-on-keys style of playing.

TRACK 56

The Tremolo

This exercise puts the tremolo where it's at home, in a bluesy setting. Keep your hand shape firm, but not gripped, and rotate quickly, back and forth like you're turning a doorknob or shaking a small can of paint, from the pinky side of your hand to the thumb side. The triple tremolo beams between note stems mean shake it, baby.

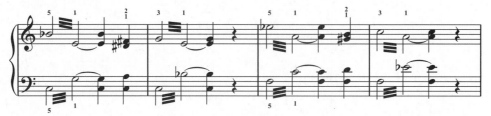

Performance Piece: "Caro Nome"

This opera aria, "Caro Nome," is well suited to vocal ornamentation, but it's refitted for the piano for this chapter's performance piece. The simple and catchy melody is perfect for dressing up with mordents, trills, grace notes, rolled chords, and repeated notes, with a little room for some turns in the left hand.

Verdi

T
R
A
C
K
57

Chapter 16

Maximum Independence: Challenging Rhythms and Syncopations

*T*he exercises in this chapter combine many of the technical elements from previous chapters to challenge your hand independence. By stretching your hand-eye synchronicity with more difficult rhythms, you get a warm-up that will leave you itching to face the greater technical challenges out there in the wide world of piano music.

In this chapter, you get practice combining scales and arpeggios with lots of rhythmic change-ups: sixteenth notes alternating with triplets; syncopated eighth notes; and contrasting rhythmic patterns in each hand.

You also get some practice with meter changes, and even some polyrhythms, with one hand playing triplets while the other plays eighths.

These workouts all feature patterns to boost your hand independence by combining scales, arpeggios, and rhythms. You can practice them slowly or at speeds to take you to the top of your form.

Let your mind guide your fingers, not the other way around. A relaxed, comfortable approach in the physical sphere of playing opens a path for the mind to think, solve, and lead.

Combining Scale and Arpeggio Patterns

The exercises in this section challenge your hand and finger independence with each hand playing an independent rhythmic part combining scale and arpeggio patterns.

Independent rhythms, scales, and arpeggios #1

The mix of sixteenth, eighth, and quarter notes keeps you on your toes.

Independent rhythms, scales, and arpeggios #2

After you have developed a clear mental picture of the patterns, up the tempo, bit by bit, to make the most of this and the preceding exercise.

Exercises with Changing Note Values

When you're playing music that changes frequently between eighth, sixteenth, and quarter notes, count sixteenth notes throughout. Doing so helps keep your tempo steady and your note values consistent.

Maintain a steady beat while playing these exercises, whether your tempo is slow or fast. Make sure you count every sixteenth note — especially those you don't play on. If it helps you to establish a steady tempo, tap your foot lightly on the quarter-note beats.

Scale patterns with changing note values

Arpeggio patterns with changing note values

Exercises with Changing Meters

When playing music that changes meters midstream, keep the underlying note value (eighth note or quarter note) the same, unless written otherwise.

Changing from 6/8 to 3/4

In this exercise, the eighth note stays the same in making the switch between 6/8 time and 3/4 time. Because the time signature changes between an eighth-note count and a quarter-note count, you switch from counting six eighth notes ("1, 2, 3, 4, 5, 6") to counting three beats of eighth notes ("1, and, 2, and, 3, and"), keeping the rate of the eighth notes constant.

Expanding and contracting meter changes

Here, all the time signatures are based on a quarter-note beat, but the number of beats expands and contracts. Count (yes, counting out loud is okay!) all the eighth notes throughout. The long and short articulations help mark the downbeats and upbeats.

Syncopation Exercises

With rhythm playing an ever-dominant role in popular music, it's a good idea to practice reading and playing syncopations, which are always harder to play than they sound. As you get more comfortable with the feel of syncopations, you can have more fun and let your music dance to the beat.

Syncopation exercise #1

Steady counting will keep you on track in this "follow the leader" exercise, as you syncopate eighth notes in first the right and then the left hand. Keep counting "one-and-two-and-three-and-four-and" throughout to anchor the exercise with a steady pulse.

Syncopation exercise #2

If you like syncopation, no better place to find it than in *montuno* patterns played by the piano in Salsa. A *montuno* is a two-measure pattern, a syncopated rhythmic and harmonic building block that, through repetition, forms the foundation of various Salsa styles. Emphasize all the syncopations — it fits perfectly in the style of the music. Give all the held-over eighths a bit of an accented push, and make sure you count the strong beat (either out loud or in your head) that's syncopated to make sure you don't clip off any of its value.

Exercises with Polyrhythms

Lucky that we are to have two hands that can play two melodies at the same time, piano players are sometimes asked to stretch their boundaries and play two opposing rhythms at the same time. One of the most common of these polyrhythms is playing two against three: for example, two subdivisions of a beat against three subdivisions. You often see an eighth-note triplet in one hand and two eighth notes in the other, or a quarter-note triplet in one hand and two quarter notes in the other. You can do the math and figure out that you play the second note of the "two" group *soon*, technically speaking, after the second note of the "three" group, and closer to the second note than the third note. Practice each hand separately until you get the feel for the pattern in each hand, and then start putting it together until the combined motion starts to feel comfortable and flow naturally.

Two in the right hand against three in the left

Start by playing the left-hand part by itself, setting a comfortable tempo and getting into a nice rhythmic groove. Then add the two eighths in the right hand, letting the left hand continue its pattern.

Three in the right hand against two in the left

For this exercise, switch the triplets to the right hand and the eighths to the left. This exercise is actually easier to play faster; after you learn the moves you'll find you can integrate them quickly.

TRACK 60

Performance Piece: "I'll Build a Stairway to Paradise"

This arrangement of George Gershwin's "I'll Build a Stairway to Paradise" features jazzy chords and syncopated rhythms. The lyrics to the song, written by B. G. DeSylva and Ira Gershwin, invite you to shake off your blues by learning how to dance, point the way to paradise by starting each day practicing, and show you the rewards of steady, step-by-step dedication. Exactly the approach needed to master the piano, I'd say. You'll get there if you keep at it, "with a new step every day."

Part V
The Part of Tens

The 5th Wave   By Rich Tennant

"Hey George, give it a rest. Let's have lunch. I picked up some bluefish. Man, I love bluefish. Do you love bluefish, George?"

In this part . . .

You get ten dance pieces to play for fun and extra exercise. I also give you ten of the best exercise collections by ten great composers.

Chapter 17

Ten Dances for Your Hands

In This Chapter

▶ Dance pieces for fun *and* exercise

▶ Melodies and rhythms of the world

In this chapter I show you ten dance pieces that will give you a ride through this world, and more piano exercises!

Jig: "Captain Jinks"

This Civil-War era tune has a lively rhythm and ornamented melody.

Calypso: "Water Come-a Me Eye"

The left hand keeps the syncopated beat going while the right hand plays in the style of steel drums, with the melody in thirds and sixths.

Waltz: "Waltz from Faust"

In this waltz by Charles Gounod, your right hand can really fly over the scales and arpeggios while your left hand keeps a steady waltz pattern.

Tarantella

This well-known Italian dance song has an irresistible rhythm coupled with a lilting melody.

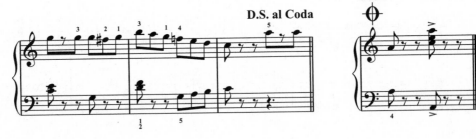

Tango: "El Porteñito"

Pay special attention to the articulations to bring out the character of this gem from the early days of the Buenos Aires tango.

Moderate Tango ♩ = 80

TRACK 66

Mexican Hat Dance

"Jarabe" means mixture, and it describes a mixture of dance rhythms, as found at the changes in the time signature. Keep the eighth note the same tempo throughout.

Polka: "Pizzicato Polka"

In this polka by Johann Strauss II, play all the notes with a short, staccato articulation to evoke the sound of violinists quietly plucking the strings of their instruments with their fingers.

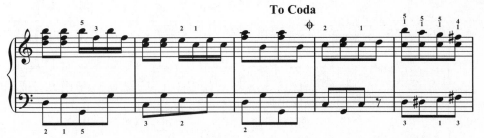

Boogie: "Johnson Rag"

Give your left hand a romp (and a real workout) with the boogie-woogie pattern that accompanies the melody in this song by Guy Hall and Henry Kleinkauf.

"Hungarian Dance No. 5"

Play the first part of this famous dance by Johannes Brahms with a strong, commanding beat, and save the dynamic surprises for the last four measures.

Moderately ♩ = 92

Gypsy Dance from Carmen

This dance by George Bizet is perfect for practicing grace notes and scale runs in thirds in the right hand.

Chapter 18

Ten Great Composers and Their Daily Workouts

In This Chapter
▶ Études and exercises by the biggies

So many composers, so little time. Both the famous and the not so famous have written enough piano exercises and études to fill your practice time, not to mention your bookshelf, with only these. The most difficult are challenging for any pianist, and many are useful to pianists at all levels. Not surprisingly, the greatest composers wrote some very difficult exercise pieces, but even if you don't get around to playing them, listening can be rewarding and instructive.

This chapter presents a selective list of some of the top collections by the top composers. If you have a local music store, thank your lucky stars and buy from that establishment. Most of my suggestions are available online at the biggest Web sites (like amazon.com and barnes andnoble.com). Here are a few stores that specialize in music:

✔ Frank Music Company: www.frankmusiccompany.com
✔ Joseph Patelson Music House: www.patelson.com
✔ Music Espresso: www.musicespresso.com
✔ Burt & Company Music Supply: www.burtnco.com

Johannes Brahms (1833–1897)

Johannes Brahms's *Fifty-One Exercises* are pure exercises, not at all performance pieces, yet they have the musicality, invention, and rigor that are the hallmarks of Brahms's writing. They're a real workout. (Published by G. Schirmer)

Frédéric Chopin (1810–1849)

Chopin wrote two books of *Études*, opus 10 and opus 25 (24 pieces in all), that cover the full range of technical possibility. More to the point, it's all incredibly beautiful music. (Published by Henle)

Muzio Clementi (1752–1832)

Gradus ad Parnassum (The Art of Playing the Pianoforte) is three volumes of piano exercises, totaling 100 pieces, in a variety of forms and styles, ranging from intermediate to advanced level. (Published by Kalmus)

Karl Czerny (1791–1857)

Karl Czerny is the king of piano exercises. He studied with Beethoven and taught Liszt — not a bad résumé. He wrote hundreds and for all levels, covering the scope of techniques used in his day. I recommend *40 Daily Exercises* (published by G. Schirmer), and if you're hungry for more exercises you can surely find something just for you in volumes such as *Studies for Small Hands*, *The Art of Finger Dexterity*, *School of Velocity*, *Eight-Measure Exercises*, *Study Pieces for the Beginner*, *24 Studies for the Left Hand*, *100 Recreations*, and *The School of Legato and Staccato*.

Claude Debussy (1862–1918)

Written near the end of Debussy's life, *12 Études* are equally beautiful and intricate studies that have titles like "For Thirds," "For Repeated Notes," and "For Octaves" (excuse my French translation), describing their technical focus. They're divided into two volumes. (Published by Durand)

Enrique Granados (1867–1916)

Six Expressive Studies are intermediate-level *estudios* and are so expressive you won't stop to think about all the exercise you're getting. (Published by Masters Music Publications)

Franz Liszt (1811–1886)

Before there were long-haired rock stars, there was Franz Liszt, virtuoso concert pianist and composer of passionate piano music that's quintessentially romantic. His *Transcendental Études* are transcendentally hard, but great to listen to. (Published by Edition Peters)

Edward MacDowell (1861–1908)

Edward MacDowell's attractive character pieces in *Twelve Studies* are fun for practice or performance. He also wrote *Twelve Virtuoso Studies*, which is more challenging but also attractive. (Published by G. Schirmer)

Carl Nielsen (1865–1931)

Piano Music for Young and Old has "24 short pieces in different keys" that do about as much as anyone would think possible with your hands in five-finger position. They're varied styles and tempos, not too long and not too hard, just right all around. (Published by Wilhelm Hansen)

Sergei Rachmaninoff (1873–1943)

In the same league with those of Chopin and Liszt, Rachmaninoff's *Études-Tableaux* shows off a top-notch technique and is complex and highly expressive. (Published by Boosey & Hawkes)

Appendix

About the CD

*T*he CD that accompanies this book is a normal audio CD that you can play in any home or car CD player, including the one in your computer.

What You'll Find on the CD

The CD contains select exercises from every chapter in the book along with the performance piece that ends each chapter. Here's a rundown of the tracks:

Track	Chapter	Exercise
Track 1	Ch. 2	Fingers one and two (left hand)
Track 2	Ch. 2	Fingers one and two (right hand)
Track 3	Ch. 2	Fingers two, three, four, and five (left hand)
Track 4	Ch. 2	Fingers two, three, four, and five (right hand)
Track 5	Ch. 2	"Come Back to Sorrento"
Track 6	Ch. 3	Legato exercise for the right hand
Track 7	Ch. 3	Legato exercise for the left hand
Track 8	Ch. 3	Staccato articulation, five-finger positions
Track 9	Ch. 3	Paganini Variation for Ten Fingers
Track 10	Ch. 4	One under two, two over one
Track 11	Ch. 4	One under three, three over one
Track 12	Ch. 4	B-flat and F-major scale passages
Track 13	Ch. 4	Aria from *La Cenerentola*
Track 14	Ch. 5	Finger combination: Two and three
Track 15	Ch. 5	Finger combinations: One and four, two and five, one and five
Track 16	Ch. 5	Exercise in fifths, sixths, and sevenths
Track 17	Ch. 5	"Take Me Out to the Ballgame"
Track 18	Ch. 6	A longer progression
Track 19	Ch. 6	Voicing chords

Track	Chapter	Exercise
Track 20	Ch. 6	Chord and melody combo #2
Track 21	Ch. 6	"Battle Hymn of Republic"
Track 22	Ch. 7	C major, C harmonic minor, C melodic minor
Track 23	Ch. 7	Varied articulation
Track 24	Ch. 7	Varied rhythmic groupings
Track 25	Ch. 7	Variation VII from "Variations on 'Twinkle, Twinkle, Little Star'"
Track 26	Ch. 8	Parallel octave exercise #1
Track 27	Ch. 8	Chromatic motion away from the center
Track 28	Ch. 8	Combination movement exercise
Track 29	Ch. 8	"Turkey in the Straw"
Track 30	Ch. 9	Broken-chord pedaling
Track 31	Ch. 9	Blurred lines and long sustains
Track 32	Ch. 9	Sustaining as the hands leave the keyboard
Track 33	Ch. 9	"Simple Gifts"
Track 34	Ch. 10	Note-to-note jumps
Track 35	Ch. 10	Two-hand parallel motion jumps
Track 36	Ch. 10	Bass-note-to-chord pattern in 4/4
Track 37	Ch. 10	"Lily Pad Rag"
Track 38	Ch. 11	Jumping thirds
Track 39	Ch. 11	Alberti bass exercise
Track 40	Ch. 11	Guitar-style broken chord exercise
Track 41	Ch. 11	"Harp Heaven"
Track 42	Ch. 12	Scale handoff exercise #1
Track 43	Ch. 12	Crossing over with the right hand
Track 44	Ch. 12	Chord "drumming"
Track 45	Ch. 12	"El Choclo"
Track 46	Ch. 13	Octave scale exercise
Track 47	Ch. 13	Exercise with longer jumps
Track 48	Ch. 13	Exercise with hand contraction and expansion
Track 49	Ch. 13	"Schumann's Octave Workout"
Track 50	Ch. 14	Diatonic triad progressions
Track 51	Ch. 14	Extended major-key chord progression
Track 52	Ch. 14	Extended minor-key chord progression
Track 53	Ch. 14	"Awake, My Heart, and Sing"
Track 54	Ch. 15	Grace notes
Track 55	Ch. 15	Mordents
Track 56	Ch. 15	The glissando
Track 57	Ch. 15	"Caro Nome"

Track	Chapter	Exercise
Track 58	Ch. 16	Independent rhythms, scales, and arpeggios #1
Track 59	Ch. 16	Changing from 6/8 to 3/4
Track 60	Ch. 16	Three in the right hand against two in the left
Track 61	Ch. 16	"I'll Build a Stairway to Paradise"
Track 62	Ch. 17	"Captain Jinks"
Track 63	Ch. 17	"Water Come-a Me Eye"
Track 64	Ch. 17	Waltz from *Faust*
Track 65	Ch. 17	Tarantella
Track 66	Ch. 17	"El Porteñito"
Track 67	Ch. 17	Mexican Hat Dance
Track 68	Ch. 17	"Pizzicato Polka"
Track 69	Ch. 17	"Johnson Rag"
Track 70	Ch. 17	"Hungarian Dance No. 5"
Track 71	Ch. 17	Gypsy Dance from *Carmen*

Customer Care

If you have trouble with the CD, please call Wiley Product Technical Support at 800-762-2974. Outside the United States, call 317-572-3993. You can also contact Wiley Product Technical Support at http://support.wiley.com. Wiley Publishing will provide technical support only for installation and other general quality control items. For technical support on the applications themselves, consult the program's vendor or author.

To place additional orders or to request information about other Wiley products, please call 877-762-2974.

Wiley Publishing, Inc., End-User License Agreement